FIELD WORK
New Nature Writing from East Anglia

Edited by Sarah Lowndes

FIELD WORK

Introduction by Sarah Lowndes
—

Bethany Settle, *The Field* 3
Bruce Rushin, *January – Stonechat* 5
Jessica D'Alton Goode, *Old Silver sliver* 6
Simeon Ralph, *A Feather From a Crow* 7
Mark Cator, *Monday* 9
Anthony Smith, *A Siskin's Song* 10
Terry Flower, *Scene from Far Off* 11
Fergus Partridge, *Window sill* 13
Fergus Partridge, *Snow* 14
David Cochrane, *Land* 15
Robert F.W. Smith, *Brief Suns* 21
Christoffelina Wuyts, *Sowing Seeds* 22
Lora Stimson, *Ash* 24
Kaavous Clayton, *Untitled* 30
Pedro Cassimo, *Her Majesty* 31
Molly Bernardin, *Post Extinction* 37
Joshua Zelos, *The High Seas* 38
Sarah Hudis, *The Sky is Like* 39
Viv Allen, *Driving* 42
Viv Allen, *Stick insect* 43
Viv Allen, *Hen* 44
Gia Mawusi, *My Land* 45
Phoebe Troup, *careful, slowly* 50
Gaia Shaw, *The Shock of Mother's Day* 51
Lindsay Nash, *Bees and Honey* 53
Donna-Louise Bishop, *Change of Seasons* 55
Scott Barton, *Snails* 57
Ann Browne, *Traces* 58

Eoghan O'Maolain, *A Lunchtime Walk* 61
Chris Mardell, *The Redwood Tree, Sequoiadendron giganteum* 62
Claire Reiderman, *Blackberry-Picking at Waxham Dunes* 64
Jason Parr, *Foraging* 66
Jason Parr, *A Place to Be* 67
Jason Parr, *Blackbird* 68
Jason Parr, *Down Sandy Lane* 69
Jason Parr, *The Reeds Give Bed* 70
Jason Parr, *The Sun Falls* 71
Rose Higham-Stainton, *Stained Pink* 72
Holly Sandiford, *Untitled* 77
Kim M. Russell, *Late Afternoon on a Norfolk Wherry* 78
Roy Ernest Ballard, *Cornish Moor* 79
Rachel Goodman, *Autumn Equinox* 80
Louise Goulding, *The Farmer's Son* 81
Lotte L.S., *Over-mind* 82
Lotte L.S., *Like Something the Light Renders Invisible* 83
Tara Sampy, *Meeting the Openness* 84
Gaia Shaw, *Untitled* 85
Gaia Shaw, *The Shed* 86
Maddie Exton, *Suffolk 'Til I Die* 87
Elizabeth Lee Reynolds, *Escape to Home* 88
Zoya Petrošiūtė, *Went* 92
Zoya Petrošiūtė, *Further* 94

—

Biographies 97
Acknowledgments 105

Sarah Lowndes
Introduction

In recent years, the climate and environment have been increasing much on peoples' minds, and this has even changed the words that we use. In 2018, the *Collins Dictionary* named *single-use* as the word of the year, reflecting the increasing global awareness of environmental issues, and the harmful impact of products (often made of plastic) used just once, only to be thrown away after. The *Oxford Dictionary* chose *climate emergency* as the most notable phrase of 2019, defining the term as "a situation in which urgent action is required to reduce or halt climate change and avoid potentially irreversible environmental damage resulting from it." Our changing vocabulary came about, to a significant extent, because of the School Strikes for Climate initiated by Swedish activist Greta Thunberg in August 2018. Thunberg's message was a simple yet eloquent one: "the moment we start behaving as if were in an emergency, we can avoid climate and ecological catastrophe." A year later, the Climate Emergency movement had swelled, leading to the largest climate strikes in world history on 20 September 2019, as some 4 million protesters, many of them schoolchildren, demonstrated across the world for immediate action to cut CO_2 emissions. Yet, while many began to modify their behaviour, for example, using a *bag for life* for shopping, buying less *fast fashion* or recycling as much as possible, still the world in general wasn't listening to Thunberg's exhortation to "act as if your house was on fire."

Since moving from the city of Glasgow to live in rural Norfolk five years ago, I have become increasingly interested and invested in the natural world. In that time, I have worked on several projects that examined the relationship between the natural world and creativity, including my book *Contemporary Artists Living Outside the City: Creative Retreat* (2018) and the shared reading and creative writing project *Like the Sea I Think* (2018–2019). The anthology *Like the Sea I Think: New Marine Writing from East Anglia* (2019) was the culmination of a year-long project, which began with free shared reading and creative writing workshops at libraries in Cromer and Norwich, and featured new writings by authors from across the region, sourced through a free to enter, open-submission call. Through the *Like the Sea I Think* (LTSIT) project, I became more aware of the widespread interest and enthusiasm for nature writing across East Anglia.

    In the winter of 2019, I applied for Arts Council England funding to develop my work with local readers and writers further. This time I extended the remit of the course readings and exercises to address not only the coast, but to reflect on the wider natural world of flora and fauna and other forms of life, found in gardens, fields, meadows and woodlands. While the LTSIT workshops had been delivered at Cromer Library and Norwich's Millennium Library, after consultation with Norfolk County Council libraries, I decided this time to work with two coastal libraries (Cromer and Great Yarmouth), to offer the workshops in areas where need might be greatest. Cromer is rated as being in the 20% most deprived areas in the UK, while Great Yarmouth is one of two local authorities in England and Wales with the smallest proportion of over-16-year-olds with level four and above qualifications (higher apprenticeships and degrees). The workshops were designed to be accessible to less confident readers and writers, as they were offered free of charge in public libraries - and used a shared reading approach, to encourage participation in personal creative expression by those who might not otherwise access creative reading and writing opportunities. The workshops ran for six weeks from the beginning of January until mid-February, aiming to offer an uplifting distraction during what is for many, the darkest, coldest and most difficult time of the year. For those who missed out on a workshop place or who lived outside the region, each week I posted the readings and exercises online so that they could follow the course remotely.

    I decided to call the project *Field Work*, in reference to Seamus Heaney's seminal 1979 poetry collection, although, as with the readings for LTSIT, I planned to use the workshops to explore some of the less obvious nature writers. My intention was to use the project to provide an opportunity to engage with nature writing written by women and people of colour, to challenge the conception of the genre as predominantly white and male. In order to show the development of nature writing as a genre, I chose to move chronologically, spending the first three meetings reading poetry: beginning with

    X—*Sarah Lowndes*

Seamus Heaney's *Digging* (1964) and *Blackberry-Picking* (1966), then Audre Lorde's poems *The Bees* (1972), *The Brown Menace or Poem to the Survival of Roaches* (1973) and *Coal* (1976) and after that, reading Mary Oliver's *Wild Geese* (1986) and *The Summer Day* (1992). We then moved on to read excerpts from three contemporary prose writers: Helen Macdonald's, *H is for Hawk* (2014), Max Porter's *Lanny* (2019) and Elizabeth-Jane Barnett's *The Grassling* (2019). Along the way, we ploughed through difficult ideological and emotional terrain, discussing environmental issues alongside and in relationship to our thoughts on class, sexism, racism, mental health and processes of grieving. *Field Work* was not only a project about reading and writing but also about how we can come together in groups, to learn together. As Audre Lorde writes so memorably in her poem *Coal*, "Love is a word another kind of open." Through our readings, discussions and sharing our writings we were able to reach new understandings of literature and ourselves. Another important part of our weekly meetings in January and February was sharing food together: to each group's six winter sessions I brought drinks, fresh fruit (satsumas, grapes, persimmons, cherries) and cheering treats like honey, fortune cookies and chocolate, to energise and sustain our work.

Each week we carried out a number of creative writing exercises designed to draw out themes and modes of expression introduced in the readings. We began with things that were relatively approachable and got more experimental as we went on. So in Week 1, we read and discussed Seamus Heaney together and then I asked the groups to do two exercises. The first was: *Write about a memory of growing something – it could be in a pot on a windowsill, in a garden or in a field.* The second was, *Write about foraging for something that grows wild – it could be blackberries, horse chestnuts, mushrooms...* In Week 2, we read Audre Lorde and then carried out an exercise linked to her poem *The Bees*: *Write about either bees or honey. Have you ever kept bees? Ever eaten local honey? Ever been stung by a bee?* For our second task, I asked the groups to move outside of their own lived experiences and consider the experience of being 'othered': *Write from the point of view of a "pest" of nature, such as a wasp, a rat or a pigeon. What is your experience of the world like?* In Week 3, after reading Mary Oliver's poetry together, I asked the groups to *Remember a time when you felt at home in nature. Describe that place – what it looked like, the sounds, how it smelled.* I then asked them if they had ever, *paid* close attention to a living creature, as Mary Oliver does the grasshopper? Can you describe what the creature looked like, and how it behaved? These early exercises were mostly reasoned from the writers' own experiences and designed to draw forth writing informed by their own wellspring of childhood and more recent memories.

In the second half of the course, our focus shifted toward contemporary prose nature writing, and I introduced techniques for writing in less familiar ways, such as using found materials, cut and paste and word association. In Week 4 the start of the Chinese Year of the Rat coincided with our meetings, in which we read an excerpt from Helen Macdonald's *H is for Hawk*, and talked and wrote about watchfulness, seeing like an animal, slowing down time and grief – with some help from the Chinese zodiac and fortune cookie mottos. The exercises for that week were: *1) Identify which Chinese zodiac animal you are. Write about that animal in a way that doesn't immediately give away which animal it is you are describing. 2) Pick words from fortune cookies. Write a text using them all.* The words the groups had to choose from included KISS, SKY, NOW, EXPECT, SOMEONE, LUCKY, MIDDLE, SOUL, HUMILITY, LIFE, FORTUNE, BAD, COMMITTEE, CROWDED, MIND, FRIEND, HEAT, HEART, ATTENTION, AGREES, CENTRE, WASTE, CRY, IMPORTANT and SEEKS. In Week 5, after reading the excerpt from Max Porter's *Lanny*, in which Dead Papa Toothwort eavesdrops on the conversations and interior monologues of an English village, we collected countryside and family sayings from the group. In Great Yarmouth, some favourites adages were: *Rain before 7, Dry by 11 / Ash before oak, you're in for a soak, Oak before ash, you're in for a splash / 1 for sorrow, 2 for joy / In April, a thousand rains*. In Cromer, colloquial expressions known to the group included: *On the huh / Red sky at night, shepherd's delight / Once bitten, twice shy / Measure twice, cut once / Pride must bear a pinch / Pearls before swine / Cast ne'er a clout 'til May is out*. Each person in the workshop selected 10 sayings they liked and then wrote a 10 line poem: each line of the poem either quoted one of the sayings or was inspired by one. We then cut our poems into 10 strips, shuffled them, laid them out in their new order and read them aloud. In Week 6, after reading excerpts from Elizabeth-Jane Burnett's *The Grassling*, we took inspiration from her poem *Eighty Yellows / for my father's eightieth birthday* (2019) and as a group composed a word association poem of all the greens we could remember seeing in recent days, which in the Great Yarmouth group

XII — Sarah Lowndes

included *fairy liquid, malachite, fir tree, moss, faded tattoo, wine gum, tussock, traffic light, screen...*

As part of the project, there were two additional free events scheduled, intended to add grist to the mill of local nature writers: in February, there was a screening of films about *Art and Place*, organised by originalprojects; at St. George's Theatre, Great Yarmouth, followed by a discussion event which I led, on artists working in the landscape. In March, there was another film screening, of Paul Wright's experimental nature documentary *Arcadia* (2018), which I organised under the auspices of Kunsthalle Cromer at Regal Movieplex in Cromer. The screening of *Arcadia* on 11th March was the last social event that I, and several of my friends and colleagues, would attend for quite some time – as in the following days social distancing measures began to be recommended in the wake of the growing Coronavirus outbreak.

On March 23rd the UK government ordered the first three-week lockdown to check the spread of the virus, after which people were only allowed to leave their homes for four reasons: infrequent shopping for basic necessities (food and medicine), one form of exercise a day (for example a run, walk or cycle, alone or with members of your household), for medical reasons (your own or caring for others) or for work reasons, when you could not work from home. The rules on daily exercise were subsequently clarified to explain that a daily run or cycle of 30 minutes or a daily walk of an hour's duration, in your local area, were considered appropriate – although the advice was to keep 2 metres distance from other people when exercising outdoors. In the warm spring weather, this proved difficult to enforce, as huge numbers of housebound people sought relief in green spaces and beauty spots. In high density areas, arguments broke out about the paucity of access to and availability of green space – and whether sunbathing or resting on park benches was permissible under the new rules.

Curiously, the recognition of the Coronavirus pandemic as a global emergency, had an immediate and positive impact on the ongoing climate emergency. With aeroplanes grounded and cars parked in driveways, global CO_2 emissions dropped markedly. Smog cleared above megacities like Los Angeles, and in Venice the canals ran clear and blue for the first time in decades. In the cities, spring birdsong was audible in the early mornings, and bats, badgers, foxes, fallow deer and otters were increasingly spotted in urban areas, emboldened by the new silence. Although it had often been said that the climate emergency would continue because people were unwilling or unable to change their behaviour, the Coronavirus lockdown proved that people could change their ways. They would work from home, they would stop travelling unnecessarily, they would walk or cycle rather than drive and they would only shop once a week for essentials. Greta Thunberg had often insisted, "Humans are very adaptable: we can still fix this. But the opportunity to do so will not last for long." In the strange spring of 2020, some positives emerged from the terrifying catastrophe of the pandemic, not least of which was the opportunity to try different approaches to how we work and how we live.

The 31st of March, a week into the first British lockdown period, was the submission deadline for this *Field Work* anthology. In that last week of March, the world had been gripped by new emotional, physical and financial challenges, not least of which was the entreaty to *stay at home*. I was delighted, then, to receive close to 80 submissions from writers across East Anglia, reflecting (somewhat poignantly) on the world beyond our windows, and the gardens, fields, rivers, broads, woodlands and beaches which make this region so outstandingly beautiful. From those diverse submissions, I made this selection of 40 writers, each of whom has something fresh and interesting to say about our natural world. 14 of the writers in the anthology attended *Field Work* workshops, but most are writers I encountered for the first time through the open submission call. Reading the new work of these writers at this time of great uncertainty, we can perhaps appreciate even more fully the power of nature to positively affect our health and mental wellbeing – and inspire us towards change.

FIELD WORK

Bethany Settle
The Field

There's this field behind our house.

I'm crouching in the living room, looking through my back door, looking through the gaps in the poorly nurtured hedge, to see the roe deer. The closest I have ever been to one.

Prop my elbows on the window sill to aid my unsteady hands with the heavy old binoculars. On a hay bale, a buzzard, still. Below, a hare in the shadow cast. These two, so close. I don't see tension, no before or after. They're just there. They just are.

We wanted to move somewhat out from the city. Space, quiet, calm, more green. We loved this house. Big 70s windows, the field behind. We got it. There was this field behind the house I grew up in. I played in it most days. It felt like an ancient place. Being in nature was leaving, forgetting. You just went away.

This field now, our field, my field, is mysterious. Surprises reveal themselves gradually. The rakish persistent little owl. A lone chicken that roosted in the hedgerow for a time last year (I called it magic chicken. Barrelling out from its perch each morning, clumsy white apparition in the blue light). Our first fancy red grouse. The stance of a wet buzzard.

When I go out walking around this bit of South Norfolk, greens and browns are richer. Trees tower, ribboning oaks menaced with ivy. The smells of horse muck and new growth and the first yellow pops of rapeseed are stronger for each choice I make. I choose to step out, I choose to step in. Drench of earth and crops and grass in the last sun of the day.

Boundaries and edges and lines keep creeping into my writing. Aged eightish onwards, I'd lie in the crops behind my house and watch the sky. Soon the tickling bugs or prickling of a rogue thistle would drift as I left myself and became everything. I made bases in hedgerows and up the woods, sanctuary places that were mine and smelt of green.

I have this fantasy, writing motif, daydream, thought experiment. I climb over the wooden bit dividing our garden hedge and suddenly I'm out there in the field. I'm in the very place that I look at every single day, out of the windows of every room that overlooks it. On the face of it, nothing happens. A woman goes into a field. Yet on some deep narrow level, something shifts and everything changes. I don't know if this is symbolism or psychogeography. Melodrama or intuition. I don't think I will ever do it, but I like to keep the idea close. It feels like closing your eyes in a patch of sun.

Where are my edges, where do I end?

There's this field, behind our house.

Trunks stripe the green in shadow and the hot clap of a pigeon's soar. Sparrows chat, hares chase, a lone magpie picks on through.

Bruce Rushin
January – Stonechat

Irresolute in January,
In this half-life,
Of the half-light,
Until, I see a stonechat,
Tiny winter caretaker of the marsh.
Perched on a single strand of sedge,
Chipping its song.
Like a gentle and precise mason's chisel,
Cutting the inscription,
'Neque lux, sine umbra'*.

*'Never light without shadow'.

Jessica D'Alton Goode
Old Silver sliver

Bright flint, cold cracked chalk
knuckled into black pitch roots,
all shining in rain.
I am cold, cracked with sad confusion
at the question of purpose
and the old contradiction between us.

Between the trees
the sky is silver,
slipping into water-soaked birches,
dripping on the shining soil.
The quiet sun shines through me
and I become part of something older.

Routines of pain-numbing
have led to dazed-living
I am learning
to stand with it, beside it
like an old friend.
Uncomfortable,
but with a hand on my shoulder.

It does not go away
but neither does the brightness.
I stand among the trees and add my shadow to their own.
The rain remembers,
I am here, is all that matters.
We are the same;
cold, cracked, and shining.

Simeon Ralph
A Feather from a Crow

First,

we meet in the barren fields behind the village. You are liquid ink spatter against parchment earth. I am breathless with the cold. You strut hunchbacked between the hardened furrows and jab your beak at the frozen ground. You are perpetual silhouette. Breathing shadow. A ragged slash on the landscape as if torn into the fabric of the air. Were I to cross the distance between us, I could reach out and push my fingertips against you and into the hole you make in the horizon and feel whatever it is on the other side. I could twist my hands into fists and hold onto it for just a single moment and then, please, just one moment more. Then, I would withdraw. I'd shake oil-black droplets of you from the ends of my fingers and back into the soil where it belongs and smear the last traces of you against the thighs of my jeans.

Instead, I am still. I am patience. I wait for you to twitch your head in my direction and when your black eyes find me we hold each other's gaze until I no longer feel the cold.

Then,

the next morning or the morning after, I find a black feather on my doorstep and know that it is yours. Its shaft is thick and cataract white. The sweeping curve of its spine points towards me and I pick it up and place the tip of it between my teeth and run my tongue over it. I anticipate the taste of soil or fungus or other things reared in the dark, but it is as clean and crisp as spring water.

I do not go to work. Instead, although it is the middle of February, I leave the front door standing wide open, walk through the house to the back door and leave that open too and wait for you.

After

the feather, you bring a coin. A glint of silver half-buried in the thin soil between where the patio ends and the lawn begins. There is so much earth ground into its ridges that the date is illegible even after rubbing at the surface with the flat of my thumb. You are not here when I find it but I know that it is yours. There is something about the way the light falls differently that tells me that you have been here. I place the coin in the palm of my left hand and curl my fingers closed around it until it is warmed. Later, I scatter porridge oats on the paving slabs in thanks.

The next morning, in the same place, there is a broken lightbulb. It is snapped into ragged teeth and, between the shards, the filament is exposed. The day after, you have left three smooth pebbles of sea-worn glass. The next, a single button, still trailing a wisp of blue thread. I never see you when I collect these gifts and line them up on display on the windowsill above the kitchen sink, but I feel that you are close. You are scrawled into my margins.

Now, I pinch your latest gift between my fingertips. It catches the sun as I tilt it towards me. An earring, plain silver and decorated only with the scrap of flesh caught within its clasp.

—Simeon Ralph

Mark Cator
Monday

He peered at that imaginable gloom crouched along the horizon. The darkness of the day was not the world he wanted to see. The butcher would have his say. Come out of the back room wiping his hands of the small traces of raw meat. "The wind has turned to the North. That will bring in the rain." And the cold he thought. "It'll be rain before the days out." Before the day's out. Before the day's in. In or out it will be raining, it always would.

The cars flickered by with boring monotony. He thought of the wood. Before the development came along. Before the, 'Breath of Fresh Air', billboards that heralded the diggers and the men in yellow jackets forever measuring and never calling the streets with the names they buried. Everything was their glorious reinvention: Queens Drive, Knights End, Maidens Close, Royalist Lane. Layer upon layer of forgetting. Not that he remembered who the Pippin was, in Pippin's Wood. He thought he did. He thought he could hold up Pippin to the rest of the world and say, here he is, this is what it's about, but now the trees of the wood have gone. The new houses grudgingly stain their place, suffocating under their own superlatives: exclusive, executive, exotic, discerning, desirable, unique and somewhere under the bonnet a piece of England was yours, identical in its difference to next door, down the road, round the crescent.

He reset the company's audio loop, 'tyres on washed pebble gravel'. She was early for her appointment. She parked in the visitor slot and stepped out in unsuitable shoes.

Anthony Smith
A Siskin's Song

Down the road the dogs start barking
By the houses behind Brick Kiln Farm.
Fresh from the east
Sleet is slopping
And a harsh wind
Means to do me harm.

'I'd spin on a sixpence
For a song', I've sung,
'Spin on a sixpence at need.'
But I haven't a song to sing,
When sleet drips down to the seed.

Terry Flower
Scene from Far Off

It was a grey overcast afternoon in February. Conducive to sitting by flaming firesides and the recalling of warm memories. But we were out. Retracing Sebald's footsteps across the arable flatlands of East Suffolk, three miles inland from estuarine Woodbridge and the site of Saxon burials. Sebald had been drawn here by stories of the FitzGeralds. In particular Edward FitzGerald, famous for his translation of the Rubaiyat of Omar Khayyam. Was it, I wondered, Sebald's admiration of the poet's craft and endeavour or FitzGerald's own admission that; *all of his relatives were mad; further that he was insane as well, but at least was aware of the fact.*[1]

Our journey began at St. Andrew's church Bredfield. A small, welcoming, narrow naved church, with a generous and elaborately carved hammer beam roof that seemed slightly out of kilter with such a modest place of worship. A *risk assessment* would have found the structure capable of bearing many times the load required of it here. A flying advertisement to a wealthy patron. From St Andrew's we set off, slip-sliding across a muddy harrowed field towards the site of Boulge Hall. It was into this manor house that the FitzGeralds moved in 1825, having previously occupied a neighbouring manor house, Bredfield House, where Edward FitzGerald was born in 1809. Nothing much remains of either great house today. The former having been hit by a flying V2 rocket in the last war, the latter decayed, and over the years pilfered for building materials. Arriving at Boulge we entered the small family church. Full of marshalled memorials to the FitzGeralds. The interior was untidy and tight. Feeling the pinch of holding too many histories. Outside the family mausoleum brooded; gothic-moody. Flint and stone in blacks and greys. Beside,

---

[1] Catherine Caulfield, *The emperor of the United States and other magnificent British eccentrics* (London, Routledge, 1981), 86.

but set apart, a long granite tombstone of polished pink Shap lifted. This the grave of Edward FitzGerald. At its head a tender homage to the poet; a spindling rose. Seeded from a Persian flower that casts it scent over the grave of Omar Khyyam. Only at this point did I feel the bud of the day turn to leaf. *Yes I have entered your olden haunts at last; through the years, through the dead scenes I have tracked you.*[2]

Moving out of shade and into the light we set off on the last leg of our field-tripping journey towards the site of Bredfield House. As we crossed scrub dotted with oaks we put up from one a roosting barn owl. It flew off to patrol a distant spinney. Up and down it went at the edge of the far leafless-grey-wood trying to flush out small birds with the silent movement of it's white wings. With perfect timing it echoed the group, trying to tease into the open-air thoughts from the day's dense thicket of experience.

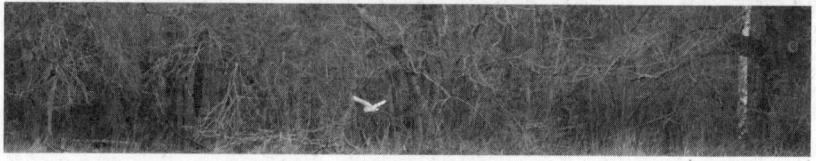

The moving finger writes; and having writ, moves on[3]

---

2   Thomas Hardy, *After the journey*. From *Woman much missed* (London, Penguin Classics, 2015), 23.

3   Omar Khayyam, *Rubaiyat*. Tr. Edward FitzGerald (New York, Random House, 1947), 35.

Fergus Partridge
Window sill

Here you are
Before me,
Propped up and beaming
On the gloss white window sill.
It's cold outside and through the nearly winter misted glass
thrushes busy themselves amongst the leaves.
The lawn has slowed for winter now.
The mower's in.
A Boeing creeps across the glass in bright silence.
I'm imagining the microscopic interior.
Peanuts and blown-up pillows,
everyone thinking only of other things.
The phone rings in the hall, but differently now:
it will never again be you.

Snow

Winter's gentle anaesthetic
is softening the details of the day.
We sleep
as a million upon a million falls –
a million silent parachutes with unplanned
planned soft landings come to cover us.
This temporary blanket
though, will turn to
mess more messy than before.
And like the drinker's nightly soporific
is the cool warmth of a promise
forever unkept –
as ready to evaporate as to solidify. Then dissolve.

David Cochrane
Land

Soil is not for growing things in built up areas. It's an all-purpose packaging material. You can sink foundations in it or cover up coffins. It is just earth, not the earth[1]

The watching sun followed the rim of a winter sky. The footsteps of our weekly escape tracked once more by this seemingly all-knowing presence. Land eventually appeared at the frayed edges of the estate. The houses, concrete and tarmac ceased and were replaced by sandy tracks rippled with gnarled roots. At this point my imagination would begin to swell like an ink-spot on the surface of my mind. We travelled far enough to free ourselves from our beginnings. Do you remember? Each walk an attempt to escape from the people we were and the confines of the estate. Outwards towards new possibilities. You, attempting to rid yourself of another week's poverty and me, outpacing beatings from bullies that made each day hell. There are no ends to meet in nature, because all ends meet quite naturally. Since you left there is so much that I long to share with you.

Your shadow at morning striding behind you
Or your shadow at evening rising to meet you;
I will show you fear in a handful of dust[2]

Nature held magic for me and with your help I could hide within it. Even though rainstorms limited our field of vision, each stick held a new potential and every hole in a hedge became a gateway to another world. You are gone now but this rough magic remains.

---

1 *The Unofficial Countryside*, Richard Mabey (Dorset, Little Toller Books, 2010), 33.
2 'The Waste Land; 1- The burial of the dead', T.S Eliot (London, Faber, 1922), 52.

As I tread thin rabbit paths deep into a corrie.
As I observe motes jostling in the amber sunbeams of a wood.
As I track the blurred and grimy fingerprints of cloud shadows floating over the land.
As I skim broad flat stones across shaded river waters.

The magic of these actions fills me with 'wild delight in spite of real sorrows'[3] not least because I am aware of my new vulnerability I am transported to a much older place, to a place before us.

However, our involvement with the land was trammelled. Each weekend we headed for 'open' land. 'Open' meant being confined to narrow pathways. Gazing out at untouchable fields, rivers and forests owned by others. Our small selection of walks were circuits. All of them removed us from the estate and the gravitational pull it possessed. Our reason for walking was never stated or needed. It was simply enough to leave. To go and be in the land, breathe the air and move within the calm that comes through the monotonous action of walking. For it is monotonous and with the feet steadily occupied the mind is allowed to float kite-like on the end of a string. The sense of 'elsewhere' continued upon returning home, not least in the tingling within our toes. The 'Countryside and rights of way act' brought the right to roam and venture freely. Too late for you and those with nothing else to call their own.

A peculiar impression comes to rest within me when out walking. It is a serenity borne of knowing I am exactly where I should be in that moment. Perhaps this is what some refer to as 'home'. For you our walks were always about returning. Your excitement at the thought of tea and a slice of toast by the fire sped up your steps. You held your corner at the bottom of the garden. Among the stands of rusting tools, beyond planted rows kept in check by sentinel canes. You dwelt in the musty air of the potting shed. Crouching upon the diminutive seat by the door with a chipped steaming cup. Frost crept across the window glass eventually bringing snow. Still you pottered. Quietly enclosing

---

3 'Nature', Ralph Waldo Emerson, *Norton Book of Nature Writing* (New York/London, Norton and Company, 1990), 147.

yourself as you dragged peace from the land.

> *Such a simple obsession may be the refuge of one's years, the desire to keep a finger in time, a brief hand in creation...or even to come to terms with one's own death. I only know that as small as my garden is I again have a living root, that even for me something can come to perfection; that I still have a place on earth*[4]

I bought you Derek Jarman's *Modern Nature* for your birthday when I wanted to show you another version of something from nothing. Of life pulled from shingle into towering form on a beach overlooked by a power station. Cracks and nooks filled with life exploding forth and belying the truth of Jarman's dwindling existence. We'd planned to travel to Prospect Cottage but that day never came. Back to the earth from whence we came. Ashes to ashes. Dust to dust.

> *I do not wish to die [...] yet, I would love to see my garden through several summers.*[5]

Your land was rented land. The land you added to your garden from the fields that lay beyond did not belong to you either. It had lay untended. 'They promised us a garden' you shrugged, with a glint in your eye. You've gone now and that land is tenanted by others. Nothing ever felt like ours. Everything rented or in the process of being paid off. House, TV, video, car, fish-tank, stereo, sofa, carpet. On and on. Never never. Rented land on rented time.

> *What are the roots that clutch, what branches grow*
> *Out of this stony rubbish? Son of man,*
> *You cannot say, or guess, for you know only*
> *A heap of broken images, where the sun beats,*[6]

—

---

[4] 'A place on earth', *Notes on the English year,* Laurie Lee (London, Penguin, 2015), 46.
[5] *Modern Nature*, Derek Jarman (London, Century, 1991), 310.
[6] 'The Waste Land; 1- The burial of the dead', T.S Eliot (London, Faber, 1922), 51.

17__*David Cochrane*

It had been late summer when we committed to our annual holiday walk along the coast path. A field enclosed by hedge reduced to stubble. Clouds approached with stealth, hiding thunder in their folds, until they sat above our heads. The first lightning bolt struck the field before us. Do you remember? I looked to you and saw panic. He remained calm and motioned for us to sit down. 'Don't head for the trees. It'll pass'. Jagged forks earthed around us, one hitting a stile on the perimeter before the augury swept on. What did we have except each other?

I'm older now and you are gone and I realise that we had walked to escape ourselves. Lost in nature's wild plan. All that is left are memories and footsteps. That's how the walking began again you see. Because of you. Using one of the first gifts you ever gave to me; the ability to walk and to know the power of putting one foot in front of the other.

A gate, hedge and hasty wooden barrier are the subject of Paul Nash's photograph 'Bledlow, Ickneild way, Buckinghamshire'[7]. The gate is jammed into the hedgerow. A few long timbers do the gate's job and the grass around the entrance sits at once flattened and tufted; the result of heavy footsteps.

The awry confluence of lines makes the image difficult to fathom. Are we looking at a hasty attempt at barricading something in or has the gate been forced and life broken through? The image unsettles me and brings you to mind, as though something within it has been undone and can never be put right.

Journeys taken across country by train and car cause my eyes to stray to the edges. Pasture bordered by hedge. Thin runnels of land between track and field, beyond which marginal creatures tread and hover. The exposed banks of dwindling rivers in high summer. I dream of departing by walking off the end of the train platform and slipping into a pool of night. Treading those borderlands appeals, partially because it is not my place. I yearn to trespass and pass beyond,

---

7 *Informal Beauty, The photographs of Paul Nash*, Simon Grant (London, Tate publishing, 2016), 24.

to quietly declare that no man can own a piece of earth or body of water. I spy places in which I would cut through a hedge or cross gates to aim for a distant horizon. These daydreams are small attempts to conjure a path, plotting a route or tracing a line.

When I showed you Richard Long's artwork 'A line made by walking'[8] you gazed at the mark heading into the distant trees and asked me where he was going. You rolled your eyes when I said that Long had said it was 'a path and yet not a path'[9] as it was 'a path going nowhere'[10].

The eye is constantly returned to the beginning of Long's line in the grass. I know you understood this return, thirsty for tea and longing for your place. I prefer his work 'As the crow flies'[11] wherein he walked in a predetermined continuous line across rolling Scottish moorland for twelve hours. I've always been fond of the term 'As the crow flies'. A line drawn from here to there. Imagining a coal-black bird in a coat of night-shaded blue skimming over stubble, clearing hedgerows with a whirr of feather to create yet another line across a field. If the crow were a messenger what message would I send to you?

I tread a line when I walk, a line traced by my finger over the whorls and rippled contours of an OS map. Maybe the yearning to take a straight line across a field is a desire to bid 'Adieu to here, no matter where'[12] and not be a 'faint-hearted crusader'[13]. To no longer join one loose end to the other and complete the circle but to follow Thoreau's encouragement and;

> ...go forth on the shortest walk, perchance, in the spirit of undying adventure, never to return.[14]

---

8   'A line made by walking', Richard Long, 1967.
9   'Interview with Martina Giezen (1985–1986)', *Richard Long Selected Statements and Interviews*, Ed. Ben Tufnell (London, Haunch of Venison, 2007), 67.
10 'Royal West of England Academy (2000)', *Richard Long Selected Statements and Interviews* (London, Haunch of Venison, 2007), 39.
11 'As the Crow Flies (23¾ miles, a one day Southward Walk in the Highlands, Scotland', 1980.
12 Arthur Rimbaud. *The philosophy of walking*, Frédéric Gros (London, Verso, 2015), 48.
13 *Walking*, Henry David Thoreau (Rockville, Arc Manor, 2007), 8.
14 Ibid.

Perhaps without you there is no home anymore, except for the clarity found on pathways adrift with autumn's shredded parchment, the open summer lightning field or the chill crack of winter on the lips, when hours have passed and the briefest envelope of daylight is closing once more.

Sometimes, often in fact, I can feel you there. It's impossible, I know. Maybe it's just a part of me carrying a part of you. It's rarely a particular walk, but a moment that snares me and I realise that you would have loved this. A glint of sunlight on waving grasses, a bubbling call of bird song, the sense of pure freedom that placing one foot in front of another can have. Freedom from myself, freedom from the past. I don't believe in ghosts or spirits but I know that you walk with me and, as I acknowledge the end of a good day, I catch your smile before my eyes and you whisper, 'It's not over yet'.

With this sense of hope for what may come it's hard to miss you absolutely. For while you are gone, you have, in these small ways, never left me.

I have always been here, tomorrow, contemplating this landscape.[15]

---

15 *A philosophy of walking*, Frédéric Gros (London, Verso, 2015), 25.

Robert F. W. Smith
Brief Suns

Brief suns:
they hang for an instant,
globes of radiant light;
then drop,
and then are swallowed up in night.
The lamp stays lit,
but soon the rain will stop.

Christoffelina Wuyts
Sowing Seeds

It must have been the spring of 1947, when I was about ten years old, that we walked to the field from our primary school to start a new project – as it would be called nowadays.

With our tools and measuring tapes at hand, we approached this North Holland's sandy soil excitedly. An icy-cold sharp wind was blowing and it felt as if it cut right through my clothes to the very bones, deeply in my body.

I had to do a lot of measuring to create a little square patch of sand, that would be mine only. I wasn't any good with straight lines, never would be, but managed it in the end. It resulted in a more or less even-sided, levelled piece of sandy earth, which was slightly raised from its little path that followed it all round.

Now I drew lines again, this time with a little twig, it made it look like a mini version of the furrows on a farmer's land. 'This is where the little seeds will go', I said to myself proudly. We had been given a precious little packet each. A kind of cress I think it was. Carefully I crumbled the seeds in the rows between what looked like little rows of sand dunes. The tops of which had now started to roll down with the movement and the dryness of the sand, covering the hoped for seedlings which were to come. I had loved that day, the exercise of doing it. Yet I was never to come back there again to see the outcome.

That night the chilling wind, which had shown its murderous strength, had beaten my immune system. High fevers plagued me, sending me poorly into hospital. Pneumonia was its name, which progressed into pleurisy and tuberculosis.

Off school for nearly a year, my sick-room was to be our garden, spending my days in bed, resting in the fresh air, residing in the living-room at night. I was very lonely, no visitors were allowed. My companions became the pear trees, the purple plums whose journeys I followed, the flowers, the birds and the bees, the little mouse that came from under the dresser at night and scuttled around my bed looking for a crumb.

Nature became my best friend, on good days and bad, with all its facets and still always is. Those seeds that were sown on that freezing day in that sandy soil, became deeply rooted in the ground, as well as in my soul, and have never gone to waste.

Lora Stimson
Ash

Winter/Spring

Seed and root wait soft underground. The earth is frozen, patches of lawn rubbed bare. The garden is a story. Nature left to itself. The arbour crushed by decades of honeysuckle bloom. The apple tree blown on its side, refusing to die. A log pile snarled by bramble, a hawthorn hedge, a chestnut sapling.

    I stand on my parents' landing, Vinny on my hip, and we look out. This is Norfolk, I tell him. A distant tractor turns the stripped earth. I point out the oak, show him the sky. Even this rigid month is orange and milk at dawn. We pause at the front window before taking the stairs. The houses across the road are shaded in sleep, dark against the whitening sky. Every morning the sound of one thing striking another somewhere out there. Soft against hard, like someone thrashing a rug with a stick. It lasts only a few seconds and then I take Vinny down for breakfast. Mum pretends to have slept, stretching arms wide. We're in a loop, both of us infinitely sad and growing frustrated with this new arrangement. The widow and the single mum.

—

On Valentine's Day it snows and the roots slow their heartbeat. Fat flakes melt on the patio. I've ordered flowers, and when they arrive Mum assumes they're for me. You shouldn't have, she says in the manner of someone who really means it. You can't win, she tells me that evening over a bottle of wine. Whatever you do will be wrong, because there's nothing you can do, she says. But please keep doing it anyway, darling. The flowers – a recreation of her wedding bouquet – sit on the hearth, dark red roses with gypsophila and eucalyptus stems. Mum won't light the fire, it was Dad who did that. Instead, she cranks the thermostat.

Daffodils bloom. Hyacinths appear blousy in the borders, tulips send up broad leaves. Cows boom low song from a distant shed.

The days lengthen and one morning I see the bashing take place. A man shucking dry mud from his boots against his garden wall. He's young, early twenties if that. He sits on his front step, pulls them on and leaves on foot. It's the same, Monday to Thursday. He arrives home as the outside light comes on timer, and leaves the boots on the porch until morning.

I paint my bedroom white, three coats to cover the grease-stains of my teenage posters. I sleep with the curtains open and in the morning the room glows. A blackbird sings loud joy from the roof. How about we put you into your own bedroom? I ask Vinny. He looks at me. Can I have gherkins for breakfast, he asks.

Mum asks about Vinny's Dad. I'm not keeping him away, I say. It's his choice. London is a far-away dream. The rumble-track of the tube beneath the basement flat. Subterranean windows and ghost-light. In London I walked to work, doubling my journey just to feel the sun on my face.

I show Vinny photographs of his grandad, and we walk along the footpath to touch the oak's thick skin. Vinny presses his cheek against the bark and I'm a child again, my arms spread, ear against the trunk, alert. Dad on its other side, whispering. Can you hear it?

Spring/Summer

Vinny's new rule: I must wait on the landing. He slams tiny heels against each step. Threenager, Mum says. Boots reverb between our houses and I watch, habit now, the familiar movement of his body. Long-limbs unfolding, slouchy gait. One morning he looks up and raises a hand. I pause, then splay fingers. Hi.

No-one told me about the apocalypse, Mum says. I'm propagating on every window sill. I dig Dad's vegetable patch over and sow beetroot, plant onion sets, bury broad beans. Mum helps Vinny grow cress in a hollow egg.

Green shoots burst. It sleets then snows. The sun shines, casting a rainbow. I show Vinny. We sing the colours and take a walk. Birds at full chatter, tender nettles crawling with ladybirds, trees in bud. We collect sticks for the fire that no one dare light. Vinny jumps pneumatic in puddles.

Each morning I watch him leave. Often, he lights a cigarette and tips his face skyward. Watching is intimate. I miss sitting on the tube. I miss looking into strangers faces. It's the only thing I miss. Though, it would be nice to go to a bar. After bashing then lacing the boots he looks up and raises his hand. I've become part of his routine.

Vinny starts pre-school and I recognise some of the mums from childhood. I eek-out awkward conversation. They want to hear about my sadness, but it feels like nothing. Like water running off a roof.

—

Every leaf is heart-shaped. Wild violet and Hollyhock. My radishes appear in tangled rows. They need thinning but I can't bear to. Everything is too tender.

I have a job remote marketing. So, you're not going back to London? Mum asks. Do you want me to go back? I say, not really an answer.

At night a fox barks and I go out to lock the coop. The chickens hear me disturbing the dew and chunter. Returning, Mum asks if I've been smoking. No, I say. I heard a fox. No, that's the muntjac, Mum says. She calls me a town mouse. I think about cigarettes.

I offer to do the food shop. On my way home he's walking on the verge. It's quarter to four. I try to convince myself I haven't planned it. I pull alongside and roll the window. Cow parsley froths behind him. Do you want a lift to the village? He shrugs and gets into the passenger seat. He smells of the ground after rain, and engine oil. You live opposite, he says. Yes, I moved home. Is that your kid? Yes, he's three. I'm sorry about your Dad, he says. He used to let me come over and use his telescope. Really? I say. Dad feels close, like he's sitting in the back seat. When I was at school I was into astronomy, he says. You're not anymore? He makes a noise and looks out of the passenger window. Do you smoke? He knows I know. Yeah, he looks at me. Can I have one? I ask.

In the church car park I roll all the windows down. A blackbird chitters a warning call and runs across the path. You moved home for your mum? He asks. I suppose, I say. Things converged. How? He twists in his seat and hangs his arm out the window. I drag on the roll-up and breathe out slow. A hoverfly buzzes into the car. Well, I say. I was on my own with a kid and Dad got ill, so. He waits for me to continue but I don't. Watch, he says, raising an index finger. The hoverfly follows the finger right to left to right, then flies away. I think they're taking pictures, I say. Or video. They're definitely aliens, he says. They're collecting evidence, I laugh. What's he called? He says. Who? Your son. Vinny, I say. Vincenzo, actually. His Dad's half Italian, but. I trail off again. But what? He says. I don't know how I want to end the sentence. But he's not interested, I say. In his own son? He asks. I make a sound. What a bell-end, he says. I laugh. Yes, I say. Proper bell-end. I let myself laugh. It feels nourishing.

    I pull up between our houses. I'm going past every Thursday if you need a lift, I say. It's not true. He nods and leaves the car, raises his hand, a familiar gesture. What's your name? I call out. He leans down to the window. Ash, he says.

Summer/Autumn

Mum's roses unfurl and Vinny wants to sniff each one. Smells like butter, he says. Mum's geraniums bleed hot pink and red, and the birds are dozy in the trees. I knock at Ash's door, tobacco in pocket. The lavender beside the door is alive with bees. I have waited for his parents to leave, and Mum has taken Vinny to visit her friend. I'm acting like a person ashamed. Ash looks baked when he answers the door. Mum says she won't light a fire because she has no kindling, I say. So I'm going out to get sticks. I wondered if want to come? Ash frowns. Why are you lighting fires in June? Because it's still cold at night and I'm trying to save her the oil. Anyway, I say, it's more of a psychological thing. Whatever, Ash says, and closes the door behind him.

    Nettles bank the path. Brambles climb high into the trees bearing tight fruit. There's a girl in my bed, Ash says. Oh, I say. He rubs his face. Are you hungover? I ask. Yep. We take the track, the mud packed hard underfoot, a hoof-print travelling in the opposite direction. My face burns and I wish I hadn't knocked at his door like I'm sixteen again. I collect fallen sticks into a bag, snapping some under my heel. Not that one, he takes it from me. There's stuff growing on that one; lichen, moss, whatever. He throws it spinning into the ditch. I feel stupid. A cloud of rooks fly over. They remind me of Saturday night in Soho. Where do you go on Fridays? I ask. Are you always watching me? Maybe, I say, flirting, maybe. I drive to college, he says. I'm doing land management. How's your Mum? He hands me a stick, shifting things. You know, I shrug. What about you? He asks. A bird replies on my behalf. Chiff-chaff-chiff-chaff. I see you running, he says. I'm terrible at it, I say. Sometimes I just run to the pig farm and sit on that stump and have a cigarette. He smiles. Or I stop and talk to Jennifer. Jennifer? The horse. That horse isn't called Jennifer, he says. How do you know? Everyone knows everything around here. Well, she looks like a Jennifer. We walk the loop, arriving home. Suppose you better get back to your girl. Better had, he says. He gives me a look that I can't decipher, and indoors I lock myself in the bathroom and cry.

—

Vinny in bed, I find Mum in the garden, smoking. I found your cigarettes, she says. She closes her eyes and turns her face to the evening sun. I laugh and she joins in, eyes still shut. Later, we open Dad's wardrobe and his scent drifts out. Having avoided it for so long doesn't make it any easier.

—

Mum hosts a party. Our neighbours cast long shadows on the lawn. I could have invited friends up from London. When he arrives with a girl I wear my disappointment like a badge. Mum's showing friends my veg patch, the tomato plants are picked dry by Vinny, who's been helping himself. I manage to avoid Ash, and slow-sink wine from a box. Mum's solar lights blink on and a few well-oiled neighbours shuffle-dance on the patio. I hide on the bench by the chicken run but he finds me. Where's your friend? I say. She's gone. Right, I say. He sits beside me. A pheasant calls in the field beyond the garden. The blackberries aren't ripe but I pluck one from the scramble beside me, crunch it between my teeth, shiver. How's Vinny, he asks. Partied out, I say. Did you hear the storm? I ask. He slept right through it.

Dad hated thunderstorms, I say. I can't stop speaking. He used to unplug all the appliances and make us turn the TV off. I pat my dress pocket for my tobacco, finding I've left it somewhere. A bat flits over us. Can I kiss you? Ash says.

Kaavous Clayton
Untitled

As the sun rises
They stir, rustle and chatter
Then rise, river-like

Overhead flutters
The swarm glides and twists as one
Splatters fall in wake

They gather at dusk
To roll and boil and murmur
Then roost in holm oak

One day they are gone
Their absence a hole above
We wait their return

Pedro Cassimo
Her Majesty

It's quite clear that H2O is two Hydrogen molecules and one of Oxygen combined into one structure, simple as that; this only reminds me that in this reality no one can or should stand alone, that we need one and other to be.

Now I'm not sure what to tell you if not invite you to my reality, where the real meets the lie, the exaggeration, the fantasy, the pleasure, the sense, the doubt, the history, the everything.

My name is an identification to whoever coexists in direct and indirect action can address me; now in my mind and heart I say John, Joao, Pedro, Cassimo, I'm all this these names in one person, soul, best to say character, for each name is an attribution to a certain reality or fantasy that I experienced and people recall it acknowledging the name they know me by during that season we coexisted.

As far as I can remember, back in Mozambique, my mum used to wake me up in the morning, soaked up by the waters that engulfed me through a deep recharging sleep, night to next day, from a sweet sometimes bitter deep sleep that took away the control or feel of my bladder, every morning I beheld the most beautiful being waking me up adverting me that I'd be late for school that I needed to get ready. Same time in the same person I understood the fatigue of watching the bed and its sheets soaked like a river and the effort to wash it by hand every day; the call was like: "John, John... acorda (wake up), acorda (wake up) filho (son)".

I was probably around 6 or 7 years old, sometimes my dad took me and my brother and sister in his yellow golden Mercedes 320Cl to school, sometimes or most of the times we took the bus to school. I can never forget the way to school as it was like entering on a new world, the car window was my cinema screen and every day was like watching a new release that you desired to watch for months. There it was a scene to never forget or to blink, sunny or cloudy, it was there standing with her mighty and power. At Her service was the Fishermen in boats or by the waters getting their fishing tools and boats ready or already fishing; some people were just walking or running by, some people were just there observing, being.

For me was like a therapy before school start, even if the day would go good or bad those moments were like a therapy, a meditation experiencing all that, the best really was the breeze and the scent that flown everywhere, it was more powerful then sleep to me, it was memory update by each second, I dwell.

I have experienced a lot more things on my time in Mozambique, somehow I have managed to save all this memory in Her Majesty (the Indic Ocean), in Her I found joy and comfort; through my time in Mozambique I saved everything in my heart and mind, if I needed to remember all of it just needed to be by Her and recall on the time that I was called John.

Bantu
So far that was it for me in Mozambique,
The land, rain and thunder prevail in me,
The more I seek and try to find
My thoughts and memory in John are confined.

I was born by the sea, from the sea I am built,
Every trip, 30 minutes, the humid salty breeze
Through my nostril to my body and soul
I sneeze the memory of each day for that I'm thankful to be

Oh you Indic, where you sending me?
What is this that I seek?
To your sister, Her Majesty the Atlantic
You send me so I can be.

"Some people want it all, but I don't a thing at all... if I ain't got you..."

Before I heard Cassimo from a brotherly voice, the last thing I recall was my mother's voice crying on land while I was taking off on the air plane to a new journey and then it was Portugal-Lisbon, the land of the sea heroes ("Heróis do Mar").

Here they called me Cassimo, Menino da Luz ("Light Boy"), the brotherhood that has more than 200 years of existence. The army boarding school was my house, my home, my ferment. I had no family there apart from my tutor which was best friend with my dad. Mozambique world was left behind in my memories, in my soul, in land, in my nostrils. It wasn't easy 7 years, during all process I spoke with my parents and family few times by phone, it was good but never enough. Obviously, I went back for holidays twice, as much as it could be afforded to me to return, I left Mozambique when I was 10. I was never forced to travel to Lisbon but yes it was agreed between me and my parents.

Summer times was the best times for I was out for holidays and could do anything that possibly I could, so whenever I could I'd reach for the sea or river and I'd take a moment to enter that world where only Her Majesty could allow me to enter, my memories of a life once lived. Going through it was like accessing your computer files instantly by a click, in this case was the flow of a humid air from the sea and the hot steam from the sun burning up high activating my senses and experiences of a blinked or a glimpse of a life once lived and loved, to a regret and thankful moment of existence. With all that going through me there she was Her Majesty standing astonishingly in front of me declaring Her purity, divine power and secrets of life, the sea.

Through Portugal I went, I did experience things that one can only imagine, I mean coming from a boy who lived once in Africa that going to Europe would be something like a miracle due to our status in society, what I mean is that not everybody has the means to just pack your bags and go to Europe; my dad had some money, but also a big family and I was lucky. Here (Portugal) I've experienced sadness, happiness, loneliness but the most a desire to go through it. The people here called me Cassimo; Her Majesty has one more episode about me.

Heróis do Mar
Oh you corner of Europa,
Oh you brave land that once met Africa,
Oh you Henriques the root of the "Sea Heroes"
Behold what you did before Her Majesty

Pedro Cassimo

Fearless you witnessed the vastness and power of Her Majesty
And to you She gave you a great honour
An honour that opened the ways
Where once one believed and many followed
I behold the Atlantic and its secrets
where the Bantu were once inmates
And you allowed the world to meet
And so, Britannia and the Heroes met.

"Em campos de glória fulge, dourados pomos brilhantes..."
"Meu principe Menino da Luz"

Fallen into a disillusion of not accomplishing the opportunity that was given to me, the door to make my family proud, the sweat and blood that took for me to have this chance, to ending up distributing pamphlets on the big Lisbon was almost like not breathing. My only door was the one of the famous island, Britannia, the land of Her Majesty, the land of Nelson, the House of Windsor.

   I had a vague idea of what to expect, to see, but at same time I was abandoning a life, dreams of a young boy, glory of the comrades, the once sacrifice that brought tears and hope to a new future to even once return to homeland and bring a change and a chance for my Mozambican fellow.

   Norfolk, I went, to its epicentre Norwich where new things came upon me like a baby first glimpse of the world, thirsty and starving to know it all I embraced it. Going through barriers and challenges I've enriched my person to the standards to continue and make a living; my dreams of going back to my motherland they were still imprinted in me, from washing dishes to bar supervisor to a health student within two years was done, although, I was in the flower of my youth plus I was experiencing the world for the first time after army boarding school and so I did fall into a sweet pit where blame, responsibility and dreams were bound to be outside the pit staring at me and I've enjoyed it so, that I did encounter the sea again. It was almost all that a young man like me or anyone could have done but not in the way I did, I decided to live and enjoy what I didn't in the past and forget all that ate me and staring, whenever fallen in to silence. Great Yarmouth was the next place, had some joys and new dreams, whenever I felt sad or reminiscent or needed meditation, I'd meet Her Majesty (the sea) and have a walk with her; she saw me at my all states, spiritually and psychologically. I had found comfort staring at the vast sea and seagulls flying by, sometimes a seal would bring her head to give a good look, I've met God there many times, sometimes I wondered why me, why I've ended up the way I did and my personal problems.

She's like a mother that endures pain and joys of her offspring, she suffers with the offspring and celebrates with too. Her silence its deeper than silence itself, for silence numbs you and brings nothing, comfort, peace or whatsoever, but the silence of the waters meeting the land its rather refreshing and nurturing in a natured way that only the soul can identify, according to the individual such experience impacts on a unique way that is memorable for the rest of the individual's life.

The beautiful Britannia statue has such a symbolic value to this particular sea and land that it's incredible, it shows epicism, glory, bravery, passion and love.

Lovers do somehow have strange encounters or disgrace, or a lace that connects them; the sea is deep indeed, deep enough for Titanic to lose itself on her deepness, but the love of two always prevailed saved by her majesty through the sinking and time. It's amazing how the sea shares many stories and tales of souls that are bound, tears of desires and despair, wishes and prayers. A human alone wouldn't stand these explosive testimony of many lives and eras.

Great is her love to us.

The Yare mouth has experienced a lot of things, it has witnessed blood and love through times and even on my time, here I'm known as Pedro, a boy from the *"Sea Heroes"* a boy descendent from the *San* from the *Bantu*, a boy known as Pedro.

This sea is a universe wonder, here at the Norfolk ground she's the Atlantic; now why would I write to you more if she can tell you everything else? Take a walk!

Britannia
Oh Great Yarmouth
Oh Her majesty have seen so much
That no man can ever match,

You know Nelson and his brave heart
You've held him tight on your bosom
And kept him and his nation prosperous as a blossom,
To the lovers and lonely you are here
Enduring your forever service by God's grace no longer I fear.
Why would I write more if you can take a walk with her Majesty.
"Still more majestic shalt thou rise"

"Do you hear me... across the waters, across the deep blue... lucky I'm in love with my best friend."

References

A Portuguesa (1890) the national anthem of Portugal, composed by Alfredo Keil and written by Henrique Lopes de Mendonça. The first line of the song is, "Heróis do mar, nobre povo (Heroes of the sea, noble people).

Rule, Britannia! (1740) is a British patriotic song, originating from the poem of the same name by James Thomson and set to music by Thomas Arne.

Alicia Keys, *If I Ain't Got You* (2003)

Jason Mraz, *Lucky* (2008)

School anthem, Colégio Militar, Lisbon, Portugal. Lyrics by General Joaquim da Costa Cascais and music by Vitorino José Peixoto.

Molly Bernardin
Post Extinction

The lonely Oceans wait
In tides and moon phases
Stars burn out in space
Eons and ages

Seas cry for company
In crashing white fists
They tsunami hungrily
Nostalgic for fish

Oceans play with rubbish
Create jellyfish from bags
Make cigarette butt starfish
Bottle lid crabs

But extinction leaves aches
Nothing else can replace

Joshua Zelos
The High Seas

Joseph Press was the Captain on Buckingham Press, a tall ship. He had a missing left eye, so he wore a dark red eye patch. However, his right eye is a piercing hard, red devil like eye. Even though he is 108 in years he looks very young and is also extremely wise. His head is the size of a potato. He prays to the devil every 30 minutes and forces torture on his crew members for disobedience. He is also suspected of being a cannibal. He is particularly dangerous because he is an immortal demon.

"Yes, I finally made my time machine after forty years! I hope I don't run into any aggressive lightning" he muttered.

"What's that?" a crew member shouted.

"We are here for the time machine, it's now", Captain Joseph Press shouted.

They ran out of the lab with their time machine, went to their ship. There were so many buttons but then they pressed a big red button...

It was WW2 the twelfth week. They ran into very cold temperatures the grey rolling clouds were worse than ever. The sea was so gloomy, and rough.

Meanwhile deep hidden in a dusty divot of a crater in the Moon, Snake Sidious lurks and sways around the earth at 2am.

Little did Joseph know of the dangers of Snake Sidious. She could transform from red to white fire when she's angry. She only gets angry when someone teases her or hurts her sons. She can only get hurt on the inside. When you say something bad it stores in her soul. People say words don't hurt but they do.

She leaps off the moon as she senses her baby but then smells smoke. She glides down to the ocean. She sees Joseph Press, praying on the boat and there was her baby in the water, what was he doing there? Did the Captain hurt him? She was boiling with rage, but she held her anger in for now.

Three billion years. Then dead silence. The universe was destroyed with fire, all you could see was fire.

Sarah Hudis
the sky is like

it's *like* living in a service station
saying my own name over and over with an
    upwards inflection

> It's like climbing out of a burning building into too much water / Or climbing out of a burning building……into a second identical burning building
> —Hera Lindsey Bird

    putting a stack of magazines in a public toilet
like giving someone your phone number
    but it's a payphone

> to be out of office, even to yourself
> —Hera Lindsey Bird

    a room of one's own
        and the walls are parentheses

like buying clothes that are too small for the
    day when you too will be small

> turn me off the grass, lock up your libraries—Virginia Woolf

        not so loud
speak in assured paragraphs

do you know what I mean

        the same / different
looking up at the big dipper under a sky *like*
    an egg pickled in tea

> perhaps they would be walking in the garden, hand in hand, or pausing on a hillside to listen to the cuckoo; or perhaps they would be skimming over miles of blue ocean in a queer little ship …. like the one in the fairy story
> —Radclyffe Hall

you might grow up to be a princess   your arms
        twist-tied
        and walk en pointe
or to kiss one and be transformed

you will laugh about this over and over *like*   *Not the well of loneliness, more like a*
   do I want to be her or cook for her   *water feature*—Hera Lindsey Bird
                       brush her hair

how to be both and   neither
  or a shoe
  or a pumpkin
  or a horse-rider
  or a politician's wife
  or a partner   *Invisible red pens... have been making*
  or a paaahdner   *their way into the middle of my sentenc-*
  or *like*   *es. I've been crossing things out every*
                     time I take a moment to think.
                     —Melissa Lozada Olivia

the pool of water that has collected in the dip
  where a tree blew over in a storm
              and tadpoles have brewed
(and by tadpoles I mean *like*   *Baby, don't make me spell it out*
the politics of ambiguity)   *for you*—Janelle Monae

  we've had to hide under metaphors for wanting
but metaphors allow for things to live that we just don't...have the words for

  it's *like* eating dessert first   *It just......comes over you, like an*
    or jumping in the sea fully clothed   *urban sandstorm/When a fish crawls up*
                     onto land?—Hera Lindsey Bird

  it's *like* I can see you   *To be silent, to be alone... one shrunk,*
indigo and *glittering* like an august evening   *with a sense of solemnity, to being one-*
  in april   *self, a wedge-shaped core of darkness*
                 —Virginia Woolf
            like a spanish bluebell   *Pink like the inside of your*
                 —Janelle Monae

like the saran plait you were afraid to get cut   *our "likes" are our knee pads, our "ums"*
                 are the knives we tuck into our boots at
                 night—Melissa Lozada Olivia

—Sarah Hudis

like maybe you're holding space
   for someone

the sky is *like*   a kind of bluey grey
   like cartoon duck eggs

it is never enough and all too much
   why can't you just make up your *like*

                          mind

*the green sand dunes with wild flowing
grasses on them, which always seemed
to be running away into some moon
country*—Virginia Woolf

Pink like the sun going down, maybe
  —Janelle Monae

*she would long to blurt this all out
to her mother, yet would stand there
tongue-tied, saying nothing at all*
—Radclyffe Hall

41—Sarah Hudis

Viv Allen
Driving

White lines on the road
White birch bark among the conifers' orange trunks
White motorway bridges veiled in green algae
White clouds in the bluest sky
White logos and lettering on HGV's
White vans,
White cars,
White lorries
White concrete like snow
White signs
White turbines rotating
With nowhere to go

Stick insect

She would stand in the palm of my small child hand

I would gently blow breath and watch her seamlessly begin to sway

Her horizontal stick body, shifted from left to right, and back to left again

Like a pendulum

The harder I blew, the faster she moved with stamina to outlast my longest breaths

It was a rocking movement

In which to hide

Hen

It wasn't so much the strewn wet feathers, the exposed innards and skeleton, although they were shocking

It was more a rhythm which slammed to a halt, an end to the call and response for which we were both needed

That morning, I called as usual while scanning the garden, holding my glance at the hen house entrance, at the base of the elder where dust baths happened and the lookout point on the log, beneath the winter honey suckle

Only on that morning did my eyes settle on scattered sandy coloured feathers beneath the apple tree, and her small torn body laying lifeless in the grass.

It's like this, a death is a death no matter how small on the outside

In that moment all my endings were wrapped in her tiny carcass

An incomplete encounter
A memory
A holding that has no shape

Heard in the fracture of irreplaceable things

Gia Mawusi
My Land

I

My Grandmother was a tall, proud African woman.
    She could barely speak proper English, like Miss Charlotte from the Mission, but she always stood up and made her way among her betters without a single notion or care about her station in society.
    She would walk on by and they would stare up and down at her with resentful eyes.
    But she did not care about them or their opinion. She was content with herself.
    That uneasy feeling of unworthiness that afterwards so many in my family felt, myself included, never once touched her soul.
    She knew who she was and where she was headed to.
    That is what I remember most about her.
    That, and her straight back, her clean and unafraid stare, that unique and loud laughter and specially, her lack of knowledge or sense about appropriateness, that later, was fiercely bestowed on us.
    I always admired her, respected her.
    I envied her freedom.
    Grandma always walked the fields with my hand tightly clasped, and she would sing, she would tell me stories about our ancestors, men that turned into lions, and how Man was connected to the Land and the Spiritual world.
    How we were all One and the Same but Different still.
    We would gather the herbs and the plants that were good for our black natural medicine, and she would teach me about which ones could save our life and which ones could kill us on the spot. Grandma would point out the animals roaming by and the places where they would hide during the scorching midday sun.
    She would teach me how to avoid the snakes and scorpions' holes and we would gather shiny rocks that looked like diamonds to take home.

I remember listening to her voice, and how she would smile back at me with a twinkle in her eye.

It was always so warm during summertime, and my back would be stuck to the cotton shirt Mama dressed me in. The sweat drops would travel from my forehead to my chin, while we made our way back to the shade of the embondeiro tree in Grandma's backyard.

After that, we would eat sitting outside on the floor, underneath that ancient tree while the heatwaves buzzed around us. And we would talk.

Later in the afternoon, Grandma would make her own tobacco, with dried leaves, honeyed by the sun and crushed to dust in her wooden pestle.

When night descended, the sky was so black, and darkness was so heavy you could feel it weighing on you like a blanket.

The stars were shiny but so distant, that they looked unreal, more like a dream. Sometimes, I thought about them as guardians watching us, looking down at us from afar.

We always slept on the floor, hard and dusty. And that smell, of tobacco, herbs, bananas, mangoes, dirt and musk, were all Grandma. They were all my childhood, my comfort, my home, an Earth, a life, a being and feeling I thought I could never find later anywhere, anymore, ever...

II

*Not something
put on the shelf to rot,
to forget
and remain forgotten...*

This country was *quite* different from my homeland.

During those first months, I was grieving badly.

I missed the sun, the heat, the never-ending view that spread before me. The yellow and tall grass where I could play hide and seek.

But most of all, I missed Grandma and our walks.

My Grandma's voice and her teachings, began to fade and I felt lost in the crowds, in the town, in the newness and difference of this new world, new people, new life.

I missed the fields. I missed that feeling of embracing the air itself, immersing in the trees and animals around us. The feeling of belonging and that feeling of connection.

I had somehow lost that.

It felt like all the smells, all the flora and fauna were different, smaller, dimmer. Not so fantastic and beautiful. Not mine.

And I grieved more than I could understand at that time. But winter came and was gone, and spring was here and suddenly, while I was walking in the grove, after months and months of numbness, feeling nothing, I found it.

It started with a whisper, pulling me deeper, and when the sounds of the town faded away, the further I went in, I began to feel it again, a glimmer, an inkling of that special space and place from before, a previous life and existence.

The grass and the weeds were growing together and making my legs itch everywhere where they touched my skin. But that whisper, that voice was calling to something forgotten within me.

A river was hidden by the trees and leaves, and its water, gurgling, running down, in circles at some places, faster and dangerously in others.

And the wind was rustling the leaves over my head and the grass, that itchiness, was there telling me something, making me pay attention, begging my soul to remember.

This place was for some reason I could not fathom, beckoning me forth.

I stepped further and sat on the trunk of the fallen tree. The skin was hard, with rough edges that imprinted in my fingers, almost hurting them. Forcing me to feel its strength, hear its pain.

I had no choice, so I just sat there and listened. And in the silence...

Not something
put on the shelf to rot,
to forget
and remain forgotten...

I heard and felt my Grandma's voice in my head, in my heart.

Not something
put on the shelf to rot,
to forget
and remain forgotten...

I almost felt her hand on mine, her smile, saw that twinkle in her eye, reminding me that nothing, nothing, nothing in life is ever lost.
　We just think it is.
　Life moves on and so must we.
　Grandma used to say that. I forgot about that, but I remember now.

Not something
put on the shelf to rot,
to forget
and remain forgotten...

Sitting there, on that fallen tree, I became quieter, stiller.
　And life happened, behind me, above me, below me, around me, inside me.
　And from that day on, I walked in that grove.
　And later, as I discovered and embraced this new land, on other landscapes as well.
　Grandma walked with me, during the hardest times in my life.
　I always felt her presence guiding me and a warmth would touch me from my core.
　And I noticed things, beautiful and simple little things I didn't before.
　I noticed the ducks, the ponds, the small deer that would come closer if I remained still. The sounds. The beetles and army of ants marching without glancing back at me.
　The blanket of connection and peace that was now wrapped around me.
　I just stayed more and more in tune with this way of observing life and not doing anything at all. Every afternoon I walked these fields so different from before.
　I kept on doing just that for no other reason than I wanted to.
　It soothed my soul.

Breathing in and out. Just breathing... Existing...
And I kept on grieving.
I kept on healing.
I kept on living.

Phoebe Troup
careful, slowly

    Imagine now, slowly,
                in case he
        comes away like a rabbit

        a loose thread walked in on
                raveling
      un to stalks of hillside,

          Imagine the needle threaded
                doling out notes as dinner
branch over under branch

as the lady gives
        same-sized square of lasagna
                as they who came before her

as the lady gives
each and every
      eye a shaping

he, no songbird
                      likely rabbit
pulling unmown loops of ribbon
pulling hair like meadows

Gaia Shaw
The Shock of Mother's Day

It happened one Mother's Day. My family had had adventures, travelled with my physicist father, to simulated Deep Space, through a mid-Atlantic hurricane, and seen the President of the USA shot dead on TV. The Gigantic Explosion on Mother's Day was domestic, personal. A moment of courage.

Sunday morning breakfast with four at the kitchen table (mother, father, two sisters), clock ticking, birds singing, it was Mother's day so there were cards and a bunch of daffodils, and a walk to look forward to, when there was a terrific blast terribly close, a volley of explosions like gun fire, a pause and the volley continued with smashing sounds.

"Duck!" yelled my father.
"What is it?" gasped my mother.

A shot, a smash, then another and another, volleys of firing from behind the kitchen.

"Someone's broken in!" gasped my sister.
We both jumped up to see what was happening.
"Stay back", ordered my dad.
"Go see." muttered my mother.

He disappeared through the kitchen door.

He shouted, "Oh my God!"

Exploding came louder, and faster, shelves creaked, crashed.
A battery of metal and glass falling "Crikey!"
kerflump "OHH NO!"
sissss "UGH!"

shards of glass "OW!"

"Are you alright? What's going on?" shouted my mother through the closed kitchen door.

My father slid back into the kitchen, and stood tussled and smeared, with a small cut to his face and on his hand. "It is not a raid. It's the ginger beer."

A ginger beer plant had been fed sugar daily, while it lived on the kitchen window-sill. My mother made ginger beer all year round, and there were always more bottles coming. She could barely keep up with the plant. We could not drink enough to satisfy the supply, as it grew ever more demanding of our consumption. No one had explained it must be halved regularly. Hers had grown unchecked.

Bottles left too long, fastened tightly fermented for months. They stood softly trying to effervesce on their shelf, then seething with vigour one at last exploded - one bottle triggering in a domino effect setting off others also full of gas. As they exploded the shelves gave way, the store cupboard was a battle-field.

That was my mum's best disaster ever. It was historic. Here was a primary introduction to fizzics and the danger of build-up of carbon dioxide.

Lindsay Nash
BEES and HONEY

Nature's sophistication reveals human inferiority when comparing the receptor sensitivities of birds, bees and humans.

For birds can see colours right into the ultra-violet spectrum and birds of prey can see polarized light and magnetic lines of force. So much more than that perceived by the human eye.

The bee colour spectrum, starts in yellow-oranges through bright blue and continues down into the short wavelengths of ultra-violet; no reds or maroons in the bee colour vocabulary. So much more than that perceived by the human eye.

These rich, luminous, yellow pigments combine with ultra-violet producing an indicator known as bee-purple which provides nectar guides signposting the way to sweetness and golden plenty.

—

The worker bee lands deftly and efficiently, guided by this very bee-purple on the petals of Black-Eyed Susan. She passes the time of day busily to'ing and fro'ing, inning and outing from one bloom and on to another, investigating, gathering, loading her saddlebag-legs with their precious cargo and pumping the nectar into her honey crop.

Later, laden and loaded, she grasps each antenna and, with her forelegs, strokes it free of pollen grains, streamlining herself ready for take-off. No excess baggage here, only vital supplies.

Against all dynamics and rules of physics, her tiny wings working so hard to gain lift and thrust, she gathers the momentum required to launch her body hive-wards, carrier of precious gold for the future generation.

She follows the intuitive senses passed to her through one hundred and twenty-five million years. From a day when a wasp first dared to feed pollen to its young, thereby crossing a wasp- to- bee threshold of evolution and bringing floral evolution with it. The evidence is to be found trapped in amber for posterity. She, however, only follows her instincts in order to survive.

She must survive. They must survive.

Donna-Louise Bishop
Change of Seasons

I still remember the way he would grab fistfuls of autumnal coloured leaves off the floor and throw them as high as possible above his head. He squealed as they rained over his body. Once they hit the ground he would pause, contentment spread across his face like jam, before crouching again for more. A walk in October would always take us twice as long.

Mud from the fields would be brought home with us, attached to our wellies. I would scream as he ran indoors, forgetting to take them off by the front door. His belly full of the Jaffa Cakes I had snuck into my pocket before we left for the walk, he would sit and wait for a much-needed juice.

By the time winter arrived, his juice was replaced with hot chocolate and marshmallows. He was more reluctant to venture outside at this time of year, unless the threat of snow hovered above our home. We hadn't had proper snow since the day he was born. That year we had to stay cocooned inside for more than four weeks. Secretly I was pleased to be safe in our bubble. I hadn't been ready to share my new status as a mum with the world quite yet.

With the little bit of snow we had been blessed with, we built a tiny snowman on the bonnet of my car. We found twigs for his arms and gravel for his eyes, mouth, and buttons. There was nothing around that resembled a carrot so we left him without a nose. Before we could discuss wardrobe he smashed the tiny snowman with his fist. Laughing he asked me to make another but as his fingers turned from pink to red and then blue I knew it was time to go inside and warm up.

As the threat of icy mornings turned into the reality of rain, crisp snowdrops appeared to greet us. Our countryside walks could start up again and I revelled in picking out a new splash suit for him. He had outgrown his last one somewhere between roast turkey on Christmas Day and a late night on New Year's Eve. I picked out a dark blue one with cute prints of tractors all over it. He hated it. That spring was spent squeezing him into the old one.

Since the introduction of Peppa Pigs, children across the globe have become professionals in the field of muddy-puddle jumping and my four-year-old would do this to his heart's content. I made sure to have a warm pair of trousers waiting on the radiator for him when I got home. This time of year we would pick a bunch of snowdrops, and later daffodils, to put in water on top of the mantle place.

Our final summer season together before the grips of school would steal him from me was spent on longer walks, smothered in sun lotions and covered in picnic remains. Instead of the fields surrounding our home, we would venture out to parks famous for their rhododendrons and landscaping. Sometimes we would treat ourselves to ice cream at the seaside.

As the sun began to set on the warmth of August, he noticed the change of seasons himself. He began asking for a light jacket before we headed outside in sandals and shorts. He would manage to stay awake just long enough to see the sunsets, like the embers of a fire. While he slept, I ironed his new school uniform for his first day, feeling the change of seasons myself.

Scott Barton
Snails

On sunny days when my friend Lu runs to my house and shouts for me through the window 'Get your bucket Roman', I know what's going on. They're cutting down the bushes!

I meet her in the back garden and we get the buckets wet and put some grass inside. Then we run to the front.

'Be careful where you step', we shout as they carry the old bushes across the pavement and into the van, 'Be careful for the snails.'

And we start to collect them up. Lu goes one side and I go the other. Big snails and little snails all looking around trying to hide from the sun. We pick them up and put them in the bucket. This is no time for play. This is serious work. Snails don't like being in the sun. They die and dry up!

And the people don't look and they step on them. We shout 'Watch out' as they carry the bushes over us. Soon all the bushes are in the van but Lu makes them wait and we pick out as many snails as we can from the branches until we've got all that we can find. Two buckets full of snails. Then we take our buckets down the hill and into the brambles where we let them out. Lu loves them so much that she lets them go all over her arms but she doesn't leave them on too long because what a snail really wants is a nice juicy berry or a cool damp spot under a rock. I don't let the snails on me but I still love them.

And then we walk back home, very, very tired from all our hard work but very happy too. And we have some juice and Lu tells me long stories all about what the snails are doing down in the brambles.

Ann Browne
Traces

'I am here out of habit'. This motto is engraved on the stone bench overlooking the circular flower bed. I wonder who suggested these words. They describe so many who visit. Of course there must be those who come by accident but most who come through the sunflower gates are frequent visitors. Some of them I recognise and many who discover the park by chance return content to have found this 'place of charm and quiet beauty'.

   The dogs are keen to get on, to run and chase their ball, impatient for their fun. I pass a tree planted to celebrate the life of 'not just a friend but a socialist friend'. Who was this friend and who were her anonymous friends who decided on this curious inscription?

   We play for a while on the old bowling green, now neglected, the once perfect lawn pitted and muddy, but ideal as an enclosed space for freedom loving dogs driven by instinct and curiosity to explore far and wide forgetting boundaries and owners. There's talk of transforming it into something but no one can decide what it could be, so for the time being it remains an unofficial dog run.

   I sit looking across the park towards the gardens of the houses on the boundary. Tall trees, one hundred years old, frame the view. Originally there were very few houses close to the park, no more than half a dozen. There would have been an uninterrupted view across open land. How the city has grown. There are other reminders of the original park. The tennis and the bowls pavilions are now locked, attractive but unused and lacking purpose. The rockery has shrunk; a great place for the young to clamber round and hide in but a far cry from its glory days. The old Anderson air-raid shelter, covered in lichen and gradually decaying, lies screened from view near the park keeper's storage huts. The sunflower gates are well travelled beginning life as part of a pagoda that was exhibited first in Philadelphia then in Vienna, next in Paris and finally in Buenos Aires. They returned to Norwich and after a number of changes found a home at the entrance to the park. Their stylised design a reminder of the now forgotten Victorian craze for all things Japanese.

I think about the people I have met here. I miss Sami and her Staffie. She came from Turkey to work as an au pair but became a dog walker instead. I'm not sure about this. I only ever see her with the same dog who she says she has adopted as her owner didn't want her. Does this qualify her as a dog walker? Is she using this term to describe her occupation or to say how she passes her time? Perhaps I've missed the humour. We talk mostly about our dogs but sometimes she tells me a little about her life. She is planning a trip in a motor home around England and Scotland with her partner and her dog. Soon, she said, but there are problems with the paper work. And then I never saw her again.

One day, while sitting on this bench I was joined by a man. He was dishevelled, wide eyed and holding a can which I was surprised to see was a soft drink. I was cross with myself for making assumptions based on his appearance. However, I was startled by his proximity as space and solitude are usually respected in this place, where intimacy is brief and controlled. Words began to pour out of him. He told me he had come to visit his sister. She lived nearby but didn't want to see him. During their childhood, somewhere in Wales, they had been close but hadn't seen each other for some time. Apparently his mother, once rich but now dead, raised spaniels and he recognised my dogs as partial spaniels. He had fond memories of the dogs of his childhood. A lot of what he said was repetitive and I grew tired concentrating, trying to follow his disconnected thoughts. I'd had a life so different to his, I thought. There was a sadness to his disordered life and it settled in the space between us, but despite that I wasn't sorry to see him move on.

Sometimes I see the twins. Their grandparents bring them almost every day. They check out the children's play area but seem happier when they are splashing in puddles and poking the fallen leaves with a stick. They run in and out of the bushes watched in that careful way that grandparents have. They stay close and copy each other. Are they developing that special bond often attributed to twins? In one way their grandfather wants this. He isn't close to his own brothers and sisters but he also wants them to have room for others. He loves these little ones so much hoping they will have perfect lives.

Late one night, too late to go into the park, the gates are closed and it is dark, I walk by the boundary railings. I glimpse movement low down by the hedge. Is it... yes it's a fox. Quite still, poised and graceful but wary it will have seen me and sensing danger it will disappear under the railings and into the park. I wish it wouldn't. The sight of a fox thrills me. Through its ability to adapt the fox brings a reminder of the countryside into this suburban space, the natural world insinuating its way back into a seemingly tamed and manicured area.

It's time to leave. I look around and admire the display of greenery and flowers. As much as I appreciate the colour and the peace I know that's not what I will think of on my way home. Instead I will think about the stories of those who have visited the park and bring it to life. It is the untidy mixture of their memories and their hopes that for me make this 'a place of charm and quiet beauty'.

Eoghan O'Maolain
A Lunchtime Walk

The avenue winds like an eel,
detached houses set back,
tended gardens,
tightly mown lawns
edged with lilac.

A narrow laneway
runs downhill,
two bollards,
a rough path
through high nettles.

This way the stud farm,
that way the river bank,
part way along a smaller,
overgrown track meanders
through tall grass.

A muddy lake,
fishermen in tents
dangle their lures.
Over the hedges,
sheep keep a watchful eye.

Chris Mardell
The Redwood Tree, Sequoiadendron giganteum

You stand imperious, weathering the storms that man and nature create.

You were born in 1840 and grow and grow, now standing 120 feet tall.

You have watched over the community for 180 years through world wars, storms and drought. What have you seen? Who have you seen?

Where do you derive your strength, your sense of purpose? Will you watch over the community for another 180 years or more, through world wars, storms and droughts? What will you see? Who will you see?

You threaten some with your strength and imperiousness. Visitors look upon you with awe. Nearby residents suggest "What if you should fall?" They would feel safer with you out of the way, nice and neat and tidy.

I sit and watch you every day. Your needles are everywhere in my life; a constant reminder of your presence.

To me, you are a magnificent creature: solid, strong, healthy and wise. Sage perhaps. You might fall, like all of us, but only when you are ready, when you are tired of life. Today you look healthy and strong; long may you inspire us with your longevity, your ambitions still ahead.

I believe you came from California all those years ago, carefully shipped to England as a mere stripling. Now we return to California, where our son lives and our granddaughter too was born.

Each year, at times you look tired. But then you shed your thousands of needles again, and weeks later your new bloom of strong bright green appears. A new sparkle about your cloak: a brilliant future that awaits.

You are a signpost on the landscape, standing tall and proud on top of Mount Pleasant and I see you from all directions as I return home from many streets. You are a signpost; an emblem of strength.

Your branches are solid, hanging heavily like thick languorous limbs. In the breeze when other trees and leaves are fluttering you remain still and calm. When strong winds blast us, you sway gently, mysteriously, at your own pace, as if reluctantly, only moving in the direction you want to go.

Goldcrests and nuthatches find food in the hair of your needles and in the soft skin of your bark. Woodpigeons and doves find security in the umbrella of your branches. Owls and crows use you as a viewing platform, to view the world from their perspective, to watch and wait for food somewhere below. The jays and squirrels love your size and endless opportunity, as a child loves a playground; thrilled by the branch they are on but always running and chasing, leaping onto the next. They bounce from branch to branch, like monkeys swinging and bouncing. Gulls and aircraft fly overhead, often on the same routes, returning to their roosts, at the same time, every day. Your height and presence is a beacon, a direction finder, an indicator of how far travelled - and how far still to go.

Your footing is solid and square; rooting you firmly to the landscape, confirming you are here to stay. Your roots, your toes, spread broadly across the ground below, and when I dig into the ground below, I find your roots spread widely up to 40 feet away.

In summer when moisture is scarce, as others expire, you stand firm, your reserves ready for another 400 years. You have seen so much, as men fight each other, through world wars, storms and crashes. The weather changes, the wind blows and the hot sun shines on, but still you endure and prosper.

What a privilege to know you, my big friend.

Claire Reiderman

Blackberry-picking at Waxham Dunes, September 2019

The sun was hot that day. One of the last good ones before the inevitable arrival of Autumn – and we had snatched it hastily, greedy for the last few glugs of the season.

Sandals hooked around our thumbs, cracked heels pushed into hot sand and with raggedy breath we dragged our laden bodies – weighted with the day's supplies (snails with shells too large for their bodies) – across the border of field and dune. We stopped for nothing; chivvied the dog when he dawdled; marching to the hazy hum of far-off farming machinery that droned across the air. Air: settled on skin damp and dusty. That sort of day, when sweat becomes a sugar-trap for thirsty flies smeared across shiny foreheads. Tiny black winged freckles flicked carelessly over your features.

We kept our sights on the slack ahead. Although the bags prised our shoulders from our bodies as they dug insistently, we never paused for the swarm of gnats. Impatient distaste: we wiped the sticky deaths from our lips. And then to cut through the panting air –

A prick /A howl.

Hannah curves over herself and takes foot in hand, upturning it to inspect her punctured sole. Brambles.

"Brambles!"

She turns back to shout at me.

I, shorter and hopelessly slower than her, am neck and neck with the piss-scavenging dog. He flicks an ear distractedly at a passing fly, unfussed by the discovery.

Brambles. We stop for nothing but brambles.

Snail shells are forgotten on the path. The dog is content in his undisturbed meanderings and cockings, we stuff the bags usually reserved for his shit full of the fat fresh fruit. I run my tongue joyously along the furry baubles and sour sweetness bursts around my mouth. Rapture. We are grinning purple grins, the stain sets in the grooves of our lips and between teeth. I puff my cheeks out and swirl the juice, eyes upwards and considering the vintage and the grape as I have seen my father do over dinner. I spread the redness over her forehead with two fingers and she does mine. We cackle and whoop, imps of the hunt.

There is a pride in foraging, a sense of some secret win. We congratulate each other on the find like explorers, or as though we have grown the fruit through many months of labour. A bird settles on a nearby branch and I squawk – flapping arms, waving hands – this is ours. She, startled, succumbs to my possessive display and settles instead on a bush of gorse. She leaves behind a feather; a trophy; now tucked behind my ear. We resume our feverish pecking.

Much later, seawater has dried to salt on our skin and shoulders itch with the rising flush of burns. There is a shiver of shade across the sand and the dog pines for his dinner.

Reluctantly we gather our scattered treasures into gaudy beach bags (and with it accidental sand that will settle stubbornly into the carpet of my bedroom floor, a reminder that the cold will pass). Dripping swimsuits, lead, half a baguette, cheap sunglasses, a yet-to-be-started novel. Reaching finally for the bags of bramble bounty, stop.

"Hannah!"

The bags, sweating with their secrets, have been torn apart by beaks as we swam. Straggly plastic reveals drupelets frothing with hatched maggots. Our stomachs cramp and the summer squirms to a close.

Claire Reiderman

Jason Parr
Foraging

This Winter Solstice,
cycling country lanes.
Eyes peeled wide for the Blackthorn's fruit.
Going slow, hunting Sloes,
Damson distractions, that keep the wheels rolling.
Hawthorn berries for the heart medicine,
keep on keeping on.
Bounty found,
soon to be pricked and introduced to the distilled Juniper.
Brown sugar and time,
shelved for the winter warmer.
A time held hug from the lug of this pretty bottle.
Sloe Gin,
I'm in,
again

A Place To Be

The Autumnal wood,
Damp days,
Shadowed thoughts,
Leaf cushions underfoot,
Moss pointing North,
Chestnuts fallen,
Both Horse and Sweet.
The smell of Fungus,
Working hard,
Breaking all things down.
The winded sounds,
Golden,
Like the lowered Sun,
Showing true colours,
In riot,
Calling loud,
'I'm home, I'm home, I'm home'.

Blackbird

The Blackbird sings an ode to nature's calling.
The song so strong, so jazz, so in tune.
A hop, skip and jump, feeding from the Earth.
The Worm's torment, the Snail's broken on stones.
Feeding its young, all fluffed up and proud.
Acrobatic flight, understanding air and wind and wing.
Choosing the Hawthorn's winter fruit , I do salute,
that red berry, held tight between that amazing yellow beak.
This is the song I seek.

Down Sandy Lane

Three Hansers, two Crows and my long shadow cast upon reed tops.
All captors of Old Sol's morning glory.
The world's turned gold and the Harrier's hunting high.
Windmills and churches, conversing of times gone by.
Pheasant scared, peasant scarred, present sacred,
In the magic of now.
Silver marshes, bronze reeds.
Jackdaws, keepers of the old mill.
Down Sandy Lane an old Oak sits,
oozing age.

Note: Hanser is a Norfolk word for Heron

Jason Parr

The Reeds Give Bed

The reeds give bed,
to the rabbit that's dead.
Laid out pretty by the water's edge.
The old Owl does swoop
and the fishes kisses ripples
for me and the rabbit
that's dead

—Jason Parr

The Sun Falls

The Sun falls,
as the fog rises,
over this cold December earth.
A chilled East wind,
shivers its rhythm,
to hungered game,
dancing upon a freshly turned
solid brown crust.
Encrusted with Flint jewels,
that holds the low gold Sun,
that reflects a gilded past,
a long shadow cast,
staggered by the broken canvas,
that stretches to a distant dead Oak,
standing tall,
a memorial to times gone by.
Peppered with Rooks,
perched high
upon the jewel-less crown,
waiting for the call
to dance a sing
their peculiar song
to which only they belong

Jason Parr

Rose Higham-Stainton
Stained Pink

> But now she is conspicuous among Lydian women
>   as sometimes at sunset
>   the rosyfingered moon
>
> surpasses all the stars. And her light
>   stretches over salt sea
>   equally and flowerdeep fields.[1]
>
> —Sappho (translated by Anne Carson)

I came back to this place—another salt sea, and flowerdeep fields—to write about us, or *the me that has assumed you, and you, and her, and them before*, and the skies are stained pink. And the air is pink, and the wall is pink and the water is pink. Nascent, born from union of floating white, derobed blue and fervent red that dares to reach out and touch—flint church, glass, wheat chaff.

Colour is wavelengths. Or more precisely, colour is stunted or long or penetrating lengths of light that we see or we don't see, as blue, violet, red, orange, each one ascertaining their own lifespan, like the flesh line on the palm of your hand. Blue light is short—it scatters like fractured artillery—collapses into mauve, violet. While red—red's spectral purity—finds its path and spreads, as if *a flower like blood blots on a page*.

It is autumn. It is winter. In the east, the air along the path that the sunlight seeks is dryer and cleaner, heaved in and out over the torn cliff-edge and fertile land—flat and broad and limitless. So that a low

---

1 Anne Carson, *If Not Winter – Fragments of Sappho*, translated by Anne Carson (New York, Vintage Books, 2002), 191.

bloated sun casts its rays. Red tips commune with aerosol mass of Cumulus, Cirrus, Altocumulus and projects something like transcendental ecstasy, spreading in saccharine. And then drains.

I rewatch old TV show credits of a blazing Californian sunset fronted by palm tree cutouts and silhouettes of surfers, montaged with blocks of azul blue sea-sky and images of sailing boats and pool houses and brilliant white SUVs. *California here we come, right back where we started from* But here California faces east and merges with the sand and shingle of Scratby to the north and Caister-on-Sea to the south, and the land's edge is puckered with off-white caravans, so that the pink is underscored by a shoal, a field, plastic. While inland, in this quiet room—fabric walls, flint rock vista—it spreads silvery over the roofs and stone crenellations, reaches a dawn peach to rose and later draws down into mauve, pales in lilac.

> [The moon is]
>   like silver [2]

Of wavelengths and meaning, and paper horizons, Etel Adnan writes—

> *Working for years in this direction led me to the suspicion that our mental world is an ongoing "translation," that perception is a translating of the object of that perception, and that any thought that we may think to be primordial, spontaneous, is already an interpretation of something which precedes it and may even be of another nature, another "stuff" than thinking itself, a wavelength, an "it" which remains unknown, a translation of this "it" by an active filtering function we call the "mind."* [3]

I translate these wavelengths—that spectral air—into pink and worry that she is a kind of osmosis (of the past) in this assignation, born of

---

2 Sappho, *Sappho – Poems and Fragments*, translated by Josephine Balmer (London, Brilliance Books, 1984). fr.112.

3 Etel Adnan, 'Notes on Unfolding Writing: the Mystic Transfer', www.asu.edu/pipercwcenter/how2journal/archive/online_archive/v1_1_1999/eanotes.html

Kleos[4]. I watch her creep—rose, vermillion, blush—marking the breaking of day, and coming of night, the copper slant of autumn, the golden renewal of Gregorian revolution. But she chooses her moments; all fleetingness. This grey morning is less a spoke than a reminder that she is not fecund flesh-flake; nor hardened earth, mother earth, stagnant bog, bosom of the home, but a rippling shadow, waning light; ungraspable, shapeshifter. Changing her clothes, all fickleness and layers. My eyes adjust and I gulp her in, sugar-high.

Rosyfingered, Anne Carson writes, *is used habitually by Homer to designate the red look of Dawn.* But Sappho inverts it—it is the moon who casts that redness. *I think Sappho means to be startling, but I don't know how startling, when she moves the epithet to a nocturnal sky.*[5]

I imagine thorny skin like flesh-hued turret-whips in the clouds or touching the serrated ridge of mountains in *Dark Mesa with Pink Sky (1930)*; time of day indeterminate. This painting is another kind of inversion, or perhaps a diversion. Georgia O'Keeffe makes the valley and clefts—the material at the centre of the painting—shifting pink; the looming mountain ridge a pitched grey and the sky—the space— an aeriated pink-coated white, as if the sun is retracting all the colour in those final throes of twilight. But it is O'Keeffe's strokes, Sappho's marks, those unknowable wavelengths, that do the work.

And then the pink pales out over the sea and a huge full moon, cut by electric cables, and I write—

Swollen and
buoyant egg
of silkened white sealed,
in anachronistic pink,
And mauven tails seeping,
into the line of blackened earth.

---

4   **kleos** plural **klea**: glory, fame (especially as conferred by poetry); that which is heard. http://sites.fas.harvard.edu/~lac14/glossary/kleos/index.ghtml

5   Anne Carson, *If Not Winter – Fragments of Sappho*, translated by Anne Carson (New York, Vintage Books, 2002), 371.

There is a moment in Claire Denis's surreal masterpiece *Highlife* (2018), set in space, where the viewer seems to enter the inseminated stomach of a girl and the camera floats through her fleshy, galactic cosmos—a misty place that spreads near infinitely to a darkness, a non-horizon. Stars puncture cellular layers of contoured air at points deepening to neon holes and we are forced to reconcile an intimate experience with an external space—*a violated womb as site of worlding.*[6]

From a becoming, to an undoing. Annie Dillard recalls the sky over her beloved Tinker Creek after a shattered star—

> *A rosy, complex light fills my kitchen at the end of these lengthening June days. From an explosion on a nearby star eight minutes ago, the light zips through space, particle-wave, strikes the planet, angles on the continent, and filters through a mesh of land dust: clay bits, sod bits, tiny windborne insects, bacteria, shreds of wing and leg, gravel dust, grits of carbon, and dried cells of grass, bark, and leaves. Reddened, the light inclines into this valley over the green western mountains; it sifts between pine needles on northern slopes, and through all the mountain black-jack oak and haw, whose leaves are unclenching one-by-one, and making an intricate, toothed and lobed haze.*[7]

Her pink sky is an active dissolution—inclining, sifting, through pine needles. Haze-making. I write, *I wonder about the potential of nothingness, to start again.*

Hours pass, or they don't. And Dillard stops on a long road trip, asphalt-blinded, for styrofoam coffee—

> *My mind has been a blank slab of black asphalt for hours, but that doesn't stop the sun's wild wheel. I set my coffee beside me on the curb; I smell loam on the wind; I pat the puppy; I watch the mountain....*

---

6   Hannah Paveck, 'No Other Voice: Claire Denis's *High Life*', Another Gaze, 27 May 2019, www.anothergaze.com/no-voice-claire-deniss-high-life-feminism

7   Annie Dillard, "Pilgrim at Tinker Creek", *Three by Annie Dillard* (New York, Harper Collins, 1990), 123.

75__Rose Higham-Stainton

The ridge's bosses and hummocks sprout bulging from its side; the whole mountain looms miles closer; the light warms and reddens; the bare forest folds and pleats itself like living protoplasm before my eyes, like a running chart, a wildly scrawling oscillograph on the present moment. The air cools; the puppy's skin is hot. I am more alive than all the world.[8]

I realise that to realise is to both awaken to and make of. At one of Colette's fictitious Parisian parties, *the light from the setting sun touched the curtains, shone through the drawing room from end to end, and Irene's friends cried out in admiration.*

'It's like fairyland!'

'The sky's going pink...'

One of them was more honest, as she took in with one glance the Seine, the old drawing-room extended by a rustic dining-room, the purple and silver curtains, the orange tea-cups and the woodfire.

'There's no justice in the world,' she murmured vindictively.[9]

Realisations can be dazzling—that there is no justice in the world, that she is more alive than all the world, that she is violated. But the reverse is also true, each pink sky near transformational; 10 December 2019, 7.34am is too wild, too intensely layered to allude some sort of meaning. *Something broke and something opened*, Dillard says, of the Creek at sunset. *I filled up like a new wineskin. I breathed in air like light; I saw a light like water.*[10]

Hours pass or they don't. I wake in her layers—brass sun, pink air, fire horizon. Move with her. Let her cloak me in her rose-coated arms and release me and dissolve—and I crouch by the window, solitary and in the world, looking out towards our future.

---

8   Annie Dillard, "Pilgrim at Tinker Creek", *Three by Annie Dillard* (New York, Harper Collins, 1990), 80.
9   Collette, "The Find", *The Other Woman – Collected Stories*, (London: Vintage, 2003), 82.
10 Annie Dillard, "Pilgrim at Tinker Creek", *Three by Annie Dillard* (New York, Harper Collins, 1990), 38.

Holly Sandiford
Untitled

She knows him
Rough skinned and khaki green
Made of blood, bones and earth

She stays completely still

He slithers over the fallen elder
Nestles himself between her legs
She knows him

Kim M. Russell
Late Afternoon on a Norfolk Wherry

His face is traced and creased by Norfolk gales,
skin tanned Van Dyke brown as wherry sails.
The wherryman sits on the tiller aft,
with steady hand he guides his graceful craft.
A waterfowl with broad vermillion hatch,
the wherry glides through reed and willow thatch,
its sail cuts dark into the sparkling light
and startles long-necked cormorants into flight.
The wherryman observes the soaring birds
scatter feathers in the sky like words.
As sundown is announced in gold and red
and other folk prepare themselves for bed,
the wherryman moors close to a windswept beach
to watch the sun slip slowly out of reach.

Roy Ernest Ballard
Cornish Moor

The bracken and the mountain ash
cleave to an open shaft.
A dropped stone makes a distant splash
as if a miner laughed
to find somebody come to see
and listen by the wild ash tree.

The wind sounds out the high-strung wire
across the tin mine moor.
Tremayne, Trevelyan, Tregire
have left for richer ore.
Their names are cut on lonely stones
to mark their foreign, Cornish bones.

The miners' digging days are done;
down are the walls they built.
There's no more metal to be won
beneath the spoil they spilt
but where they spat their apple seeds
green apples grow among the weeds.

Rachel Goodman
Autumn Equinox

cut lavender stalks catch fire   /   sizz
    between my ears
        flare at their ends
and I am fragrant   /   rushing into flame

I borrow smoke   lifting its wings   /
little ash flakes rise
    settle on me   /   I am a speckled egg
        ringed in the field   my brain in holes

a pale blue dome
    pecked open into silky cups   /   I am
        a fallen rose   weakened by a month of rain
petals mashed into the slug-sticky earth

my skin
    is not smoke   /   shell or soil
        my boots press my weight into the earth
            heavy as / dew

Louise Goulding
The Farmer's Son

My dad was the farmer's son,
treading neat tilled lines at four
broadcasting wheat; swinging left
and right the metal pan:

One for the rook,
One for the crow,
One to rot
And one to grow;

Dad had four of us – all daughters,
never met the oldest two. And now
I eye my little sister, wondering
which of us will grow?

Lotte L.S.
Over-mind

After H.D

Otherwise on waking :: something about :: the top of the hill :: honeysuckle conferring in the breeze :: where she climbed her first tree :: where in a potentially sooner rather than later :: but distant nonetheless :: future :: she wanted her ashes to pollute :: spore :: the Original One had scoured the same spot weeks earlier :: failing to find the tree :: no matter what had been laid to rest since :: the two of them tied through an invisible spool :: she had taken to calling the Original One late-night at weekends :: to checking for flies in the light fixtures :: hiding razors under the sink :: to feeling so much of so little :: elsewhere :: the Original One was attending circle council at 9.30 :: from 10.30 to 14.30 was free to roam :: the undulating fields :: excesses of green :: no phones allowed :: nothing to shake off the dust :: it's so beautiful here the Original One commented over instant-message :: then went off without intent :: at 15.00 all were instructed to create a life-lodge :: whatever that might look like for you :: groups splintered off :: the Original One wandered :: wondered :: settling on a fallen trunk :: the fluency of light began to gnaw :: anything that had felt at all certain :: receded :: a wholeness refracted :: the hollowed-out areas of wayward roots :: perpetual chlorophyll living :: a caterpillar chewed on a leaf :: three moths flung themselves to the ground :: the tissue around the site of damage altered :: revised its edges :: at 18.00 groups clustered :: the Original One told a story which was to be mirrored back :: a tree focused largely in the story :: the Original One could not remember which type of tree exactly :: but did remember the smell :: the touch :: the unearthly comfort it could have :: if for one glorious nanosecond :: the Original One would not think :: of him

Like Something the Light Renders Invisible

And he climbs back into the car. The sudden jolt
before falling asleep. Sun frisking every cell goodnight.
Zero phone calls home. A deception
in which the sleeping body initially appears to be
dead. She can feel the forces but not yet see their teeth.
The sycamore slumped over the car like an arrestee. She thinks
about coming. She thinks about going.
Among the diminishing amounts of available light. The ear
hears what the eye no longer detects. The eye sees what
the ear remains dormant to. Skin regains all possibilities
for uncertainty. Slight loss of breath.
A sensation of extension. The shuttering of the eyes to imagine
oneself elsewhere. Each passing thought similar but not
the same. On opening.
The axis of a tree shifting to become an arrow pointing east.
A duck looking to the left suddenly a rabbit gazing
upwards. The inability to distinguish the faintest flicker of sunshine
on the face. Like leaving the projectionist's
at daybreak. Nevertheless.
She is able to differentiate the tree as sycamore. Through
the air currents alone streaming in from the window.
The deciduous sycamore. Freshly enucleated. Abandoned fridges
stretched out like sunbathers at the side of the road.
All that's left—
two names scratched onto a single cell of bark.
Awaiting elucidation.

Tara Sampy
Meeting the openness

So I've managed to get outside
Tightly packed in
Zipped up down
Hood up
Hat hidden beneath
Gloved and scarfed

In the familiar
Cold wind I walk
My walk
Seeking the open edge to
Breathe into
Underfoot
I'm tentative
Careful on the loose ground
Fearful on the inside

Be out. Find.

There they are, trembling in the oncoming
Broken bits
Torn
Defiant but weakened by
Weak spindles
Clutching their seed
Still standing
Holding on to
Last year's energy

Taking myself forward
Finding strength in the open edges

Gaia Shaw
Untitled

take care of the hope
for a future when
the girl
has no
subject
and the satellites
and the family
have
moved on

The Shed

The shed is not a death in life
Please don't go there never to return
The shed is where you must pass through in order to come home

Do not be afraid of sleeping in the shed
As long as it is summer
Away from compost, not near the paraffin

The shed is where water falls this way or that off the roof
I want to go with my back and my heart and eyes and my hands
Not with the flow of the traffic

I shall take my self
To the shed
And eat peas and draw the trees of the orchard

The season will come home to me
Because I am in the little shed

Maddie Exton
Suffolk 'Til I Die

Born and bred,
Here I wander,
Here (my parents roof I'm under).

Born and bred,
Death by boredom
Suffolk in my blood, post-mortem.

Born and bred,
Working people,
Local Co-op: my cathedral.

Born and bred,
Culture deprived,
Trapped at home if you can't drive.

Suffolk is my first and last,
Extons present, future, past.
Fact is; I love village gossip,
Buried here
(and that's a promise).

Elizabeth Lee Reynolds
Escape to Home

In many works of nature writing the ability to leave home is almost taken for granted. Often readers follow the lone male as he picks his way through an inspiring wilderness. In Kathleen Jamie's collection of essays, *Sightlines*, she fights this stereotype. Not only is she one of few female nature writers but she also often brings other people into her accounts. Whether friends, colleagues or new encounters she acknowledges their contribution to her journey.

However, she also seems desperate to shake off the domestic, the homely reassurances, perhaps fighting the stereotype of the female figure. She bobs between the remotest Scottish islands, finding locations further and further cut off, almost inaccessible at times. There are serious physical, particularly meteorological, limitations to her trips, and yet, she makes it. To islands in the middle of the sea, miles away from other human life, amenities or, if needed, rescue.

While one part of me longs for this disconnection from the modern world, the ability to lie at night and feel almost engulfed by the sounds of nature around you, the crash of the waves, the calls of creatures, the unrivalled immensity of the clear night sky, another part cries out in fear.

A few years ago, this latter cry was a consuming part of my existence. Anxiety, the less well acknowledged but perhaps more abundant cousin of depression, can be a paralysing condition, making even short trips a struggle. Every day gripped by fear, locking you to the confines of your home. This in itself creates further conflicts. As you become more and more enclosed even going for a simple walk around the neighbourhood seems like a terrifying adventure and yet you know the well-documented mental health benefits of getting out into nature.

Short drives to the shops, let alone drives further along the A12, to the unknown haunts of Thorpeness or Aldeburgh would result in uncontrollable panic. Waves of fear would paralyse my body. I'd feel the overwhelming need to turn back, escape the situation. I felt like my body was on the verge of giving up on me, abandoning me to ridiculous, unnecessary terror. This was my life a few years ago but I was eventually able to overcome it, though the remains of an anxious mind still means I am held back from living fully. I struggle to go on walks much more than an hour long. I still have a need to remain in close proximity to the safety of home or at least an easy route back there.

Anxiety and panic disorder are very odd things. They are at once a link into our natural instincts at the same time as being a battle against them. Richard Mabey in his *Nature Cure*, a book where he documents his recovery after a serious depressive episode and his journey discovering a new home, describes how we "evolved as talkers and dreamers". It is this ability which is "our niche" that sets us apart from the rest of the natural world but it is also how we remain connected to it.

Mabey says that "language and imagination have to some extent deadened the quickness of our sensual relationships with the outside world" and yet it is this uncontrollable imagination which creates the abstract fears that lead to anxiety, which taps into an almost animal instinct within us. The fight or flight reaction is what creates a panic attack, an instinctive reaction to danger. But the dangers are often just figments, or at least overreactions, to our overactive imaginations.

The reminders of those panics still creeps within. An unhelpful fear of the fear, which never manifests in anything but makes any new experience or trip that much harder to face. Venturing outside of my known habitat still feels more uncomfortable than it should.

I'm not alone in feeling a need for the security of home. Amongst many others John Clare, the peasant poet of the Romantic period, felt a deep connection and need for the stability of his home in Helpston. The significant changes seen to the countryside surrounding his home during his adolescence resulted in a sense of dislocation which likely contributed to him being institutionalised later in life.

One of his early poems, named after his beloved village, intimately demonstrates the grief he feels at how enclosure and a drive for profit has destroyed his source of retreat. The final stanza denies the idea that anyone can be happy anywhere but home, and that their heart will always yearn for that place:

> *So when the traveller uncertain roams*
> *On lost roads leading every where but home*
> *Each vain desire that leaves his heart in pain*
> *Each fruitless hope to cherish it in vain*
> *Each hated track so slowly left behind*
> *Makes for home which night denies to find*
> *And every wish that leaves the aching breast*
> *Flies to the spot where all its wishes rest*

The struggle for Clare to settle anywhere away from his childhood home is expressed throughout his work. When he was committed to an asylum in Epping Forest his desire to return home led him to walk the whole journey back over several days. He found himself back in Peterborough but this place, just 3 miles away from Helpston, did not feel like his home either. His move there some years earlier had left him feeling lost and unable to connect to even the familiar birds and trees he found around him.

But the modern world requires a bit more flexibility on defining home. In my life I've called five towns and cities across two countries home, and a handful more have acted as alternative sanctuaries. Whether being uprooted in the first decade of life to a different country has made me more adaptable to calling a place a home or given me the need to cling to one, I'm not quite sure.

Making a home is not a quick process. You need to embed yourself in the place you find yourself in, dig deep and let it take hold. Having moved to Colchester from Woodbridge a few years ago I now call this my home. The long history of Colchester and living in the shadow of the Roman Wall helped establish a strong connection but still every now and then there is a sense that I'm not quite at home, and I need to return to the comfort of Woodbridge that acted as a nest while I battled with my mental health.

As well as the history of the town I also bring the quiet and unassuming natural life of Colchester into my daily life. The buzz of bees in the blossoms outside my house. The birds in the park. Foxes bickering in the night. The restoring abilities of these simple everyday interactions cannot be undermined but I still long for more. The impulse to seek it out, however, is often muted by a fear of the "bigger" nature, not only in its remoteness but also its overwhelming majesty. A fear of the power of emotional responses. Even the grand Essex skies can sometimes feel oppressive.

It was the same lurch of fear which grabbed me when I first looked over Rydal Water after climbing up one of the hills surrounding it. It was perhaps one of the smallest hills in the Lake District so the climb had not been physically challenging but a mental push. Every few yards a feeling like a line pulling around my stomach nearly made me turn on my heel and head back for the safety of the car. But I persevered.

Pausing and looking as the grandeur of the landscape unfolded around me, I felt relief and joy to have made it this far. The water of the lake below reflected back the perfect image of the hill on the other side. In the distance the more impressive peaks gleamed as dusk began to fall. Halos of golden light beamed through breaks in the cloud, picking out sunny spots of greenery among the light, pattering rain.

I smiled, glad to be able to experience and embrace this beauty. Grateful to have made it on a journey that would seem insignificant to many but for me represented a leap forward. The need to escape melted around me, replaced by a desire to stay. I felt at peace and safe, even though my home was over 300 miles away.

Zoja Petrošiūtė
Went

The tourists went.
The sun closed the seagull's eye slightly.
A pebble coast –
wet guipure barely touches my feet –
the sea longs for its mermaids.
Waves, swaying
seagulls,
follow every girl sadly.
Greyish and greenish girls disappeared
two thousand years ago.
And still the sea has been waiting,
will wait another two thousand years.

Išvyko

Išvyko turistai.
Saulė primerkia žuvėdrai akelę.
Akmenukų pakrantė –
šlapias gipiūras vos paliečia pėdas –
jūra ilgisi savo undinių.
Bangos – žuvėdrų sūpynės –
liūdnai palydi kiekvieną merginą.
Pilkšvos ir žalsvos mergaitės išnyko
prieš du tūkstančius metų.
O jūra vis laukia
ir lauks dar du tūkstančius metų.

Further

A starling sees me,
the light of his eyes penetrates my own pupils.
The starling's eyes
turned into juniper berries –
the bird flew away –
his eyes remained to watch further.
A little drunken worm emerged from a sour raspberry
and quietly crawled to live on.
Small waves run towards the shore of the river,
then the wind chases them on the grass.

Toliau

Mane pamato varnėno akys –
jo akių švieselės įduria į mano akių vyzdžius.
Varnėno akys virto kadagio uogom –
paukštis nuskrido –
akutės liko stebėti toliau.
Iš surūgusios avietės išlenda girtas kirminukas –
takeliu nušliaužia gyvent toliau.
Mažos bangelės nubėga link kranto upe,
paskui vėjas jas gena žole.

Biographies

SARAH LOWNDES is a writer, curator and lecturer. Research Fellow at NUA, Lowndes also contributes to the Public Programme of the Sainsbury Centre and works with the education team at Time and Tide Museum. Her publications include *Contemporary Artists Working Outside the City: Creative Retreat* (2018), *The DIY Movement in Art, Music and Publishing* (2016), *All Art is Political: Writings on Performative Art* (2014) and *Social Sculpture: The Rise of the Glasgow Art Scene* (2010). Her editorial projects include co-editing with Andrew Nairne *Actions: The image of the world can be different* (2018) and co-editing with Nell Croose Myhill, *Site Writing* (2020). Under the auspices of Kunsthalle Cromer, she curated and produced *Panoramic Sea Happening* (2017), *Esplanade: A Procession for Women* (2018) and the writing and publication project, *Like the Sea I Think* (2019).

VIV ALLEN is a visual artist who lives and works in Norfolk. Having studied 3D design in Brighton, her practice has developed to include moving image, photography and the written word. Since completing her MA in Fine Art, she has been working on collaborative projects using word and image.

ROY ERNEST BALLARD (b. 1932) lives in Norwich. He was evacuated in 1939 to Newlyn East, Cornwall from East Ham, London. A professional chemist (B.Sc., Ph.D, D.Sc.) he worked at the United Kingdom Atomic Energy Authority, Harwell (Senior Scientific Officer), taught at various universities (Oxford, UEA and Tucson, Arizona) and authored technical books and papers. He served 11 years in the Territorial Army.

SCOTT BARTON lives in Norwich, likes being in cold water, is a writer. His writing often focuses on the adventure and discovery found in small moments. He writes about living with a body and a mind, and learning how to allow them to be and to grow and change.

MOLLY BERNARDIN grew up in West Sussex, and studies Scriptwriting and Performance at the University of East Anglia. She is interested in the relationship between literature and activism, especially using literature to create a safe space for experiencing disaster.

DONNA-LOUISE BISHOP is a regional journalist and creative writer. Mum to three noisy boys, she enjoys writing micro and flash fiction and is currently editing her first novel. She is an MPhil student at the University of South Wales and graduated from Glamorgan University in 2007. She can usually be found in rural north Norfolk with a cuppa in hand.

ANN BROWNE likes open spaces, gardens, plants, animals and people. She is beginning to enjoy writing creatively but reading remains her first and enduring love.

JOÃO PEDRO CASSIMO is a Portuguese natural of Mozambique, Maputo, born in 1990. He moved to Portugal in 2000 to attend Colégio Militar army boarding school. He moved to England in 2008, where he studied Health and Social Care Lv. 3 Health Studies A levels. He moved from Norwich to Great Yarmouth, where he worked in factories, catering and studied music, and also became active within the community, performing in events and organizing community projects.

MARK CATOR is a photographer and set up UtterBooks in Great Yarmouth in 2018 with the purpose of developing a hub for photography in the East of England. Previously he worked in photojournalism.

KAAVOUS CLAYTON is a designer and maker of social interventions and situations. He is co-director of originalprojects; a charity that uses contemporary art to uncover, support, create and promote cultural assets in Great Yarmouth where he lives and works.

DAVID COCHRANE is a writer, born in Manchester and living in Norwich. He is currently working on a collection of essays and stories to be published in late 2020.

JESSICA D'ALTON GOODE is a Norwich-based illustrator/artist who finds she sometimes wishes she was a musician – or a filmmaker – and who has grown to greatly appreciate the value of poetry. And also dark chocolate hobnobs; milk chocolate are simply not as satisfying.

In her own words, *MADDIE EXTON* makes things and makes things happen. In other words, she is a conceptual artist and writer based in East Anglia. She was awarded a scholarship to study Fine Art at Norwich University of The Arts, graduating in 2020.

TERRY FLOWER graduated from Goldsmiths College in 1986. His practice engages with fine art and creative writing. 'My work is a prompt, encouraging the exploration of the landscape around us; One does not need an exotic location to begin, it's out there in the most ordinary of places happening every day.'

LOUISE GOULDING lives in Norwich with her husband, their son and their second-hand cat. Her work has appeared in anthologies from Mother's Milk Books and the 2019 Olga Sinclair Prize collection. She was commended in the 2014 Words And Women competition, and in the Mother's Milk Books Writing Prize 2016.

RACHEL GOODMAN is a poet, painter and gardener living in North Norfolk. She has an MA in Creative Writing from UEA. She has been published in *Ink, Sweat & Tears*, *Writing Places* and *Like the Sea I Think* (UEA Publishing Project) and has won or been shortlisted for several international competitions including the Bridport Prize 2017.

SARAH HUDIS is a creative-critical writer from Aberystwyth, now based in Norwich. Her work has been published by Seam Editions, Poetry Wales, and in the anthology *Like The Sea I Think: New Marine Writing from East Anglia*.

LOTTE L.S. is a poet living in Great Yarmouth. She keeps an infrequent newsletter, *Shedonism*.

ROSE HIGHAM-STAINTON writes about arts, literature and popular culture, focusing on women's creative practices. She has a Masters in Writing from Royal College of Art and has work held in the Women's Art Library at Goldsmiths College, and published in *MAP Magazine*, *NOIT*, *The Pluralist*, *Dazed Digital*, *LOVE* and *V Magazine*.

CHRIS MARDELL lives in Norwich; an occasional artist he worked as a surveyor for 40 years in London and East Anglia. Currently trustee of the Norfolk Contemporary Art Society, formerly Chair of the Peterborough Sculpture Trust, he was a founding trustee of Vivacity Culture and Leisure Trust, and winner of Arts and Business Individual of the Year 2007.

GIA MAWUSI is a writer currently living in Great Yarmouth, East Anglia. She was born in Mozambique and grew up in Lisbon, Portugal. Gia writes poetry and fiction mainly in Portuguese, English and uses idioms from her native dialects Sena and Ndau. She is currently working on her first novel.

LINDSAY NASH maintains the belief that nature and the elements provide therapy and perspective and are life's panacea. As an educationalist, working with adults and children alike, she keenly links this with literacy and creativity in order to facilitate their learning. She lives in Norfolk and also enjoys writing and illustrating children's stories.

EOGHAN O' MAOLAIN was born in Dublin city and spent his childhood near Dalkey, on the south side of Dublin Bay. He moved to London where he worked and studied. He is married with two children and has lived in Norfolk since 2006.

JASON PARR is a self-taught sculptor, musician, poet. Born in Gorleston, Norfolk in 1970, the youngest of 4 siblings. He has two children: a son, 21 and a daughter, 3 years old. He has produced two poetry albums, *Soup* and *Bubble and Squeak* which you can hear on Bandcamp.

FERGUS PARTRIDGE graduated with a degree in fine art from Camberwell School of Art. He then founded, and was Creative Director of London design agency, theFarm. He now specialises in brand identity design, illustration and copywriting, working independently in Norfolk.

ZOJA PETROŠIŪTĖ does not consider herself to be a poet; writing is rather a hobby, a therapy, the way to catch a moment and express it. Zoja was raised in Lithuania, but she was born in Belarus. She lives in Great Yarmouth now and works with an organisation to support migrants in the town.

SIMEON RALPH has an MA in Creative Writing from MMU and his short fiction has appeared in several publications both online and in print. He is also a musician with the DIY noise-rock band, Fashoda Crisis. Originally from Essex, he lives and works in Norwich.

In the tradition of the low-country 'strangers', CLAIRE REIDERMAN left Belgium to resettle in Norfolk in 2013, swapping one flat landscape of waterways for another. After finishing her degree at UEA she continued a love affair with the region, where she remains to write stories and walk her dog (who is very happy to be included).

ELIZABETH LEE REYNOLDS is a writer currently based in Essex who primarily focuses on themes of place and environmental politics. She has featured in various publications including pieces in anthologies by Wivenhoe publishers, Dunlin Press, and *The Ecologist*. She also spends much of her time supporting community and environmental activism.

BRUCE RUSHIN studied for a BA Hons at Ravensbourne College of Art, after which he taught art for many years. He was the designer of general circulation £2 coin (1998–2016) and Sailing 50p for London Olympics 2012. Retired, he is now producing artwork, primarily prints, concerned with our relationship with nature – and experimenting with ways to integrate images and text.

KIM M. RUSSELL has written poetry since she was at school. Since retiring from teaching in 2014, she has created several poems a day, and has been published on-line and in print: *Afflatus Magazine*, Peeking Cat Anthologies, Chiaroscuro (dVerse Poets), *Anthology of Aunts* and *Second Place Rosette* (Emma Press).

TARA SAMPY lives in North Norfolk with her husband and two daughters. Nature, place and meaning are key interests in her work and she has exhibited regionally, nationally and internationally. More recently she has rekindled her delight in printmaking and walking and is playing with plants and ink on paper.

Nature is where *HOLLY SANDIFORD* would find magic as a child and solace as an adult. Being part of the *Field Work* project helped her to begin to put this connection into words.

Since completing UEA's Creative Writing Prose MA in 2007, *BETHANY SETTLE* has worked for the Norfolk library service and a woodland burial park. Currently a school librarian/careers facilitator and writing a novel, she lives in South Norfolk, and appreciates the skylarks every day.

During Covid-19 lockdown, *GAIA SHAW* is keeping company with her mother at her childhood home, planting vegetables (beans, leeks, parsley...) and keeping a *Journal of the Pandemic Year*. Her submissions to *Field Work* are about everyday courage, resilience and hope for the future, and were written before 2020.

ANTHONY SMITH enjoyed a career in archives administration and historical research with the Historical Manuscripts Commission and The National Archives. Now retired, he works as a volunteer archivist and continues to publish learned historical articles. Although he has written poems since childhood, this is the first time one has been published.

ROBERT F. W. SMITH is an aspiring novelist studying Prose Fiction at UEA. He moved to Norfolk from Southampton in 2014 after completing a PhD in History. Weather and landscape have always been among his main inspirations, along with astronomy, music and the past.

LORA STIMSON grew up in Essex and studied at Norwich School of Art & Design. She has recorded words for BBC Radio 4 and sings, appearing on Luke Wright's EP *Twenty*. She's currently writing a novel and is represented by Blake Friedmann Agency. She lives in rural south Norfolk.

PHOEBE TROUP is a British-American poet and musician, born in Bristol and raised in Colorado, US. In 2017 Phoebe received her BA in English Literature with Creative Writing from the UEA. Her debut EP *Sungbetween* was released in October 2019.

CHRISTOFFELINA WUYTS was born in The Netherlands in 1936. A childhood marred by family tragedy and wartime occupation led her to find solace in nature. Remnants of people's lives found on bomb-sites, made her think; tenacious flowers finding their way through rubble, inspired her. She moved to England in 1958, settled in Norfolk in 1975. After retiring from nursing, she later worked as a psychotherapist. Member of a poetry group, she now concentrates on her memoirs.

JOSHUA ZELOS is a Year 5 pupil at St. George's Primary in Great Yarmouth. He wrote *The High Seas* as part of an intervention writing group run by Clare Parker at Time and Tide Museum, with the aim of inspiring pupils to write. The group explored the museum, wrote in different locations and discovered objects and art to use as stimulus for story settings and characters.

Acknowledgements

Field Work was supported using public funding by Arts Council England. We gratefully acknowledge additional support given by Norfolk County Council Libraries and UEA Publishing Project.

Thanks to the staff of both Great Yarmouth Library and Cromer Library who supported the delivery of the *Field Work* shared reading and writing workshops in January and February 2020.

Thanks to the Great Yarmouth and Cromer Library Field Work workshop participants: Viv Allen, Bev Broadhead, Ruth Brumby, Mark Cator, Kaavous Clayton, Grace Edwards, Rose Higham-Stainton, Pamela Kilgour, Lotte L.S., Patricia Jane Lee, Ligia Macedo, Cate McKay Haynes, Tom Lamprell, Miranda McKenna, Lindsay Nash, Jason Parr, Zoya Petrošiūtė, Simeon Ralph, Claire Reiderman, Bruce Rushin, Tara Sampy, Holly Sandiford, Angie Smith, Nic Smith, Jeana Simmons, Victoria Stewart, Karl Trosclair, Gloria Webb and Charlie Wilson. It was a pleasure to read and write together with you all.

Zoja Petrošiūtė would like to acknowledge Lotte L.S.'s helpful contribution towards the translation of her poems *Went* and *Further* from Lithuanian to English.

Thanks to all those who have encouraged the project with advice and friendship: Anna Cook, Julia Devonshire, Lucy Ducker, Leigh Ferguson, Joe Hedinger, Nathan Hamilton, Henry Jackson Newcomb, Philip Langeskov, Henry Layte, Andrew Miller, Nell Croose Myhill, Katie Nicoll, Lizzy O'Brien, Kay Pallister, Oliver Payne, Gordon Robertson, Vicky Rutherford, Becky Thomas, Samantha Walton, Jonathan P. Watts, and most of all, Raymond Wright, Richard Wright and Violet Wright.

FIELD WORK
New Nature Writing from East Anglia

Edited by Sarah Lowndes

First published in this edition by UEA Publishing Project
with Kunsthalle Cromer, 2020
International © 2020 retained by individual authors
Selection © 2020 Sarah Lowndes

This book is sold subject to the condition that it shall not, by way of trade or
otherwise, be lent, resold, hired out, stored in a retrieval system, or otherwise
circulated without the publisher's prior consent in any form of binding or
cover other than that in which it is published and without a similar condition
including this condition being imposed on the subsequent purchaser.

Design and typesetting by Emily Benton Book Design
Proof-read by Nell Croose Myhill
Printed and bound in Estonia by Tallinn Book Printers in an edition of 500

Distribution by
NBN International
10 Thornbury Road
Plymouth
PL6 7PP
t. +44(0)1752 2023102
e. cservs@nbninternational.com

ISBN 978-1-911343-92-9